WINGS
IN THE
WILD

WINGS
IN THE
WILD

Habits and
Habitats of
North American
Birds

photographs by Tom Vezo
text by Paul Kerlinger

STACKPOLE
BOOKS

To our mothers, Stella Pistorino and Betty Kerlinger,
and to our brothers, Joe Vezo and Stephen Kerlinger.

We thank them for sharing the same love
of the outdoors and nature that we do.

T. V.
P. K.

Photographs copyright © 2001 by Tom Vezo
Text copyright © 2001 by Paul Kerlinger

Published by
STACKPOLE BOOKS
5067 Ritter Road
Mechanicsburg, PA 17055
www.stackpolebooks.com

Printed in China

On the cover: Least Tern (Sterna antillarum)
Cover design by Tracy Patterson
Interior design by Beth Oberholtzer

10 9 8 7 6 5 4 3 2 1

First edition

Library of Congress Cataloging-in-Publication Data

Kerlinger, Paul.
    Wings in the wild : habits and habitats of North American birds / text by Paul Kerlinger ;
photographs by Tom Vezo. — 1st ed.
        p.   cm.
    ISBN 0-8117-2989-3
    1. Birds—Behavior—North America.   2. Birds—Habitat—North America.   I. Vezo, Tom.
II. Title.

QL681 .K47   2001
598'.097—dc21
                                                    00-058374

Contents

Acknowledgments

I'd like to acknowledge the following people for their help, support, and friendship through my years of birding and photography. First, I'd like to thank Dorothy D'Amato, my best friend, who supports my photography unconditionally and has helped me achieve some great images. Also: Arthur and Elaine Morris—it was Elaine's death that made me realize that life is too short to be working at something you don't enjoy; this in part made me change my career. May she rest in peace. My good friend Arthur Morris for his enthusiasm, support, and encouragement for my photography. Pat Lindsay, who I first started birding with and spent many years exploring the country. George Mitchell, who shares the same love of photography that I do. I thank him for his words of wisdom and encouragement. All of the birding publications that used my photos and articles and encouraged me to go on, Gordon Van Woerkom, Eldon Grejj, Diane Jolie, and Greg Butcher at *Birder's World*, Bill Thompson III at *Bird Watcher's Digest*, Tim Gallagher at *Living Bird* magazine, and June Kikuchi and Amy Hooper at *WildBird* magazine. Also, Don and Lillian Stokes, authors of Stokes Field Guides. Sharron Cohen Powers, former owner of The Wildlife Collection, my first stock agency. Doug Wechsler and Bill Matthews at Visual Resources for Ornithology (VIREO). My friends at Nikon, Dave Gardner (who was my photo buddy for years), Joyce Gerrits, and Jim Crawley, for helping to expedite my equipment through the Nikon service department. Bill Pekala and Lindsay Silverman for their knowledge of Nikon equipment and Bill's help in attaining new and borrowed equipment through Nikon Professional Services for the times I really needed it. Joanne Donnis, my assistant, who, before I moved to Arizona, ran my office in New York while I was on the road. And to all my photographer and birding friends, too long to list here, in Long Island, New York, and across the country. And lastly, to the people that made this book come to fruition: Paul Kerlinger for being so easy, accommodating, and fun to work with; Mark Allison, editor, and the staff at Stackpole Books for their interest, insight, and cooperation with this project.

T. V.

I thank Jane Kashlak, my best friend, for encouraging me to write and for providing valuable insight. I also thank Clay and Pat Sutton and the many other birders who have helped me learn about birds. Finally, I greatly appreciate the editorial assistance of Mark Allison and the staff at Stackpole Books.

P. K.

Introduction

BIRDS ARE BEAUTIFUL, WHETHER YOU LOOK AT THEM BY THEMSELVES OR WITH OTHER BIRDS. THEIR colors and shapes are what first catch a birder's eye. After that, we notice their movements and watch what they do. Finally, we take in the entire picture: bird, behavior, and setting. Together, these elements capture our imagination, draw us in, make us want to see more.

Bird-watchers differ in what they like to observe. Some love the color and quick movement of songbirds in the trees. Some love to watch seabirds gliding above the waves. Some wait patiently to see hawks soaring over a mountain, shorebirds probing a beach, or a huge flock of waterfowl landing on a lake. Although the birds are beautiful by themselves, the fact that they behave in the context of a habitat and interact with other birds makes them more intriguing and exciting to watch. Seeing the birds in their natural element, doing what they do to thrive, makes us appreciate them all the more. Sometimes, such scenes can be breathtaking.

This book is about birds behaving in their natural settings. It is about the habits of birds and the habitats they occupy. For a growing number of birders, it is not enough to know what species of bird they are looking at, or whether the bird is adult, immature, male, or female. As birding matures and birders become increasingly sophisticated, there is a growing need among us to know more about the biology of birds. We want answers to questions about the hows and whys of bird behavior. We want to know details about the adaptations birds have developed to survive in the wild.

In this book, we present photographs of birds in specific situations. Each picture tells a story about the bird's life: specifically, what it is doing in a certain setting—feeding, flying, courting, nesting, calling, hiding, resting. Although each of the photographs tells a tale by itself, we provide brief descriptions of what the bird is doing, and why it's behaving as it is. The stories focus on specific aspects of the birds' lives: their habits and habitats. The behaviors illustrated and discussed vary greatly, and, of course, each one is only a small aspect of a given bird's existence. Together, the photographs and descriptions will help readers understand what they are seeing when they make observations in the field.

The organization of this book is by biome and habitat. Each chapter covers either a biome (a biogeographic area), a habitat type, or a mixture of the two. The distinctions we have made for the different habitat types are, in some cases, a mix of these two ecological concepts. Although they do not always adhere to ecologically correct terminology or principles, the habitat categories are recognizable to birders as places where they will find particular birds. The terminology is similar to that which is common among birders.

We have chosen to distinguish between birds that live part or most of their lives in the arctic tundra; forest and field; desert, scrub, and prairie; freshwater habitats; ocean and sea; and the seashore. Although these habitats are easy for birders and naturalists to understand, it should be remembered that most birds change habitats during the year, and sometimes with only a few wing beats. Peregrine Falcons nest on arctic cliffs and move along Atlantic beaches to their winter home near tidal wetlands in Venezuela. Black-crowned Night-Herons nest in the forest and forage in the salt marsh or along riverbanks. Bonaparte's Gulls nest in trees of the Canadian subarctic and migrate to the edge of the ocean, spending the winter at sea. Each of these birds changes biome and habitat several times during the year. The amazing ability of birds to adapt to different surroundings is one of the things that fascinates bird-lovers and makes birds so interesting to study.

The birds in this book represent an array of species found throughout North America. They also represent a diversity of habitat types and behavioral characteristics. We hope that the photographs and text of this book will help birders and other nature-lovers gain a greater understanding and appreciation of birds. We hope that they, like us, will not only be taken by the beauty of the birds and their habitats, but will also be awed by their behavior.

Arctic Tundra

WELL TO THE NORTH OF WHERE MOST PEOPLE LIVE IS A LAND THAT EXPERIENCES ENDLESS DAYS IN summer and endless nights in winter. The arctic is what ecologists call a biome, within which the habitat is primarily tundra. It is a mostly treeless setting, where only inches beneath the earth's surface lies a thick layer of permanently frozen ground called permafrost. Most of the tundra is covered by grasses, sedges, and other low vegetation that is often wet, if it's not frozen. Much of the tundra is rocky and sterile, dotted with patches of lichens and mosses. The few trees and shrubs that grow on the tundra are dwarfed, generally not more than a foot or two high. Occasionally, especially along river valleys, which sometimes extend well above the Arctic Circle, the trees are taller.

The arctic tundra shares some features with deserts, grasslands, and prairies. All have low rainfall. On the tundra, however, there is little evaporation, so the precipitation that does fall is not lost quickly, and it generally stays near the surface, above the underground layer of ice. This is why much of the tundra is muskeg, or mushy ground.

The arctic tundra habitat extends around the top of the globe, including parts of Siberia, northern Europe, Greenland, Canada, and Alaska. It is a vast and sometimes inhospitable area. In the winter, little food is available; as a result, few birds live there all year long. In late spring and summer, however, the arctic explodes with life, and the arrival of hundreds of thousands of songbirds, shorebirds, waterfowl, jaegers, and raptors transforms the landscape. The migrants arrive just after the winter ice melts and terrestrial insects and aquatic invertebrates begin to become superabundant. This wealth of prey forms the bottom of a food chain that supports most of the arctic's nesting birds.

These birds are adapted to the almost violent changes of weather and season common to the arctic tundra. Because there are few tall trees, they mostly nest on or near the ground. Most arctic nesters are migrants, spending only one, two, three, or, at most, four months of the year in northern latitudes. During these months, they mate, build nests, lay eggs, raise young, then leave. Some individuals, especially among the shorebirds, don't even raise young; they simply mate and then head south, leaving another of their species to incubate the eggs and, sometimes, tend to the chicks.

At the end of summer, most of the birds in this chapter can be seen at more temperate latitudes. After leaving the tundra, the migrants' lives change quickly, as adaptations for living in warmer, even tropical, environments are needed for survival.

Like many birds that nest in open habitats, the **Pacific Golden-Plover** has developed effective strategies to deal with predators, including the broken-wing display, shown here. When a predator is near a nest or young plovers, a parent will feign injury by dragging a wing across the ground and move away from the nest, all while vocalizing to hold the predator's attention. The display continues until the predator—often an Arctic Fox or Long-tailed Jaeger—has been led a safe distance from the nest. Birders most often see golden-plovers during migration and rarely get a good look at the brilliant gold markings on the bird's back. After mating and nesting, the plover molts into its drab winter plumage and has little need to display its colors so vividly.

The **Arctic Tern** spends more of its lifetime in daylight than practically any other bird. Its nesting grounds on the treeless arctic tundra or temperate northern islands offer nearly twenty-four hours of sunlight during the summer—this bird was photographed at midnight. As winter approaches, the bird flies to well south of the equator to enjoy another summer of long days and short nights. Seldom seen from the shore, the Arctic Tern is one of the most pelagic of terns, spending most of its life on the open ocean. Its existence is one of almost constant movement; it migrates farther than practically any other bird, covering some twenty thousand miles a year. Individuals tracked on radar as they initiated migratory flights have been observed climbing vertically at a steady rate of just under three miles an hour to several thousand feet above the water. The details of its life at these altitudes remain unknown.

The **Pacific Loon** at right sits on a nest only a few feet from a shallow freshwater pond near Churchill, Manitoba. These birds also nest along the banks of lakes in the arctic tundra and southward into the taiga, the transition area between tundra and boreal forest. Loons come ashore only rarely during the year, mostly during the two and a half months it takes them to lay eggs and raise young. They spend most of their lives in the water. On land, their short legs set far back on their bodies, which make them such powerful swimmers, barely allow them to stand up or walk. The splashing combined with vocalizations made by the loon above seem to be a signal to bring in its mate. A predator, in this case a jaeger, was flying overhead. If left unattended, this loon's offspring would be a prime target for arctic predators like jaegers and foxes.

Even before its field marks are seen, the powerful and rapid flight of the **Peregrine Falcon** identifies it. In migration, its flight is usually direct; it appears to be in a hurry, flapping steadily or flapping then gliding intermittently. Along the east and west coasts, many peregrines fly at relatively low altitudes, often only a few yards above the waves or dunes. They do not hesitate when they encounter water and can be found many miles offshore. Most migrating peregrines seen along the U.S. coasts nest on arctic cliffs, often near a coastline or river. The bird is thought to be one of the fastest living organisms, capable of dives in excess of a hundred miles an hour.

With its nest surrounded by a luxuriant ground cover of Lapland rosebay, this **American Golden-Plover** seems comfortable while it broods a nest. Although snow may still be on the ground when the plover arrives at its arctic nesting site in late May or early June, the bird will soon have nearly twenty-four hours of daylight in which to forage and feed its young. At this time of year, insects become plentiful. Although nesting on the barren tundra environment makes the plover's eggs and young easy prey, the advantages of the arctic's long days and almost unlimited food supply help explain why these birds return to the tundra each year to nest. Getting to the arctic from its wintering range in South America is no easy task, however. The golden-plover's migration covers more than four thousand miles.

Snowy Owls are arctic nesters, most at home in wide-open spaces, away from trees and other things that break the horizon; they prefer to perch on the ground, especially on slightly elevated sites. This immature male is perched on a sand dune on Long Island after migrating fifteen hundred or more miles from where it hatched only five months earlier. On the Canadian Great Plains, where a majority of these birds winter, the Snowy Owl is usually found in flat, open farm fields. When it ventures south into tree-covered regions in the United States, however, it must perch on sand dunes, electric poles, rooftops, and the like to get a clear view of its surroundings. Unlike many owls, the snowy hunts in both daylight and darkness. Its hunting strategy is, most often, to sit and wait for a vole, mouse, or other bird to pass within striking distance.

Perched at the top of a dwarf willow near Nome, Alaska, a **Yellow Wagtail** sits quietly, pumping its tail up and down—a behavior that gives it its name. This bird is poised to take off and fly straight up in the air to more than seventy feet before slowly descending back to earth—a lively aerial display used to attract a mate and advertise its territory. This display behavior is similar to that of Horned Larks and other grassland nesters, probably because the wagtail's home is similar to the grasslands—low tundra vegetation seldom more than two or three feet high.

The **Red-necked Phalarope** (*left and above*) is among the most aquatic of shorebirds, spending much of its time swimming in search of food. On occasion, it swims in circles, which apparently creates a vortex, trapping invertebrates and making them easy to capture. The phalarope's lobed feet act as paddles, an adaptation that makes the bird especially at home in the water. The species also can trap air around its breast feathers to increase its buoyancy—an adaptation lacking in most shorebirds, which cannot stay afloat for long periods of time and therefore do not land on the water. Phalaropes even copulate in water, further demonstrating the degree to which they spend time in their chosen medium. Role reversal is not uncommon among shorebirds. Female Red-necked Phalaropes are more brightly colored than the males, and males are often left to incubate the eggs.

The eerie call of the **Red-throated Loon** can be heard at nesting ponds across the Canadian and Alaskan arctic or when the birds gather, or stage, prior to spring migration. It is not uncommon to hear Red-throated Loons calling from just beyond the surf line at Cape May, New Jersey, and other places along the east coast from February into April, just before they return to the arctic tundra. Like most loons, Red-throated Loons lay their eggs in nests only a few feet from the water and only inches above water level. The loon at right is turning its eggs at its nest near Nome, Alaska. Because incubating birds can warm only the side of the egg closest to their abdomens, there is a danger that one side of the embryo could lose too much heat, killing the developing chick. This is particularly risky for loons because they nest on the tundra, where the ground never holds much heat. By turning the eggs, loons keep the entire embryo warm.

Singing from a "high" perch on the tundra of northern Alaska, the **Arctic Warbler** advertises for a mate with a thin, trilling call. Although it is sitting on the tallest tree in the area, it is only ten feet above the ground. Arctic Warblers are found almost invariably along moving water or lakes, the only places in the arctic where small patches of "larger" trees can be found. Arctic Warblers are actually Old World warblers and are not closely related to North American wood-warblers. Instead, they are more closely linked to Old World flycatchers. Arctic Warblers that nest in northern Alaska are an extension of the Siberian population. Unlike the wood-warblers that nest in Alaska and migrate into Central and South America, Alaskan Arctic Warblers migrate into Southeast Asia.

It may seem strange to see a gull in a tree, but a more bizarre sight is a gull sitting on a nest in the top of a black spruce in the Canadian north. **Bonaparte's Gulls** are one of the few species of gulls that nest in trees, and they often do so well away from water. Tree nesting is probably an adaptation to avoid predation that would result if these birds nested on the ground like virtually all other gulls. After leaving the partially forested wilderness of its low arctic–taiga nesting area, the Bonaparte's Gull migrates to the ocean, where it spends the remainder of the year. This dramatic habitat shift is one of the most marked in the bird world.

Bluethroats are among the most colorful of arctic-nesting songbirds, but they are more secretive than this photo suggests. They usually scamper around on the ground, where they nest and forage, often on mountain slopes and arctic tundra. In North America, the species is limited to northernmost Alaska, not far from the Bering Land Bridge, the prehistoric route which once connected Asia to North America. The time Bluethroats spend in Alaska is limited to only about three months of the year. Like a few other birds that nest in the Alaskan arctic, such as Northern Wheatears, Arctic Warblers, and Yellow Wagtails, Bluethroats migrate out of North America and into southeastern Asia after nesting.

Summer is a time of abundance for birds nesting on the Canadian tundra. This male **Smith's Longspur** has just caught a large insect larva, a choice morsel for its mate or young. This bird's nest is a short distance away, on the ground under a large rock, concealed from predators and protected from wind and rain. The microclimate created by this location shortens the nesting season by reducing the energetic needs of chicks. In the fickle weather of the tundra, cold temperatures, rain, and even snowfall during the nesting season demand that calories be expended keeping warm instead of growing. By selecting a protected microclimate for its nest, this longspur has insured the fastest growth possible given extreme climatic conditions.

The hawklike bill of the **Northern Shrike** is a clue to the bird's predatory nature. Because the shrike doesn't have strong feet and talons like a raptor, it must use its bill to both kill and tear the flesh from the small birds and mice on which it preys. It uses thorns and barbs to impale its prey as it tears it into bite-size pieces—a behavior that allows the shrike to secure and eat prey despite its relatively weak feet, and which has earned it the somewhat lurid nickname "butcher bird."

Whitewash on a cliff face is a sure sign of a raptor or raven nest. This **Gyrfalcon** eyrie near Nome is a traditional nesting site for both ravens and Gyrfalcons; generations of birds have stained the rocks below the site a permanent white with their excrement. Biologists searching the arctic for Gyrfalcon or Peregrine Falcon nests simply look for whitewashed cliffs as they fly low over the tundra. In some areas, every suitable cliff is occupied by a Gyrfalcon, peregrine, or raven nest. Gyrfalcons often do not build their nests; instead, they look for the stick nests built by ravens or Rough-legged Hawks. They begin nesting at these sites earlier than any other arctic species.

Nesting on grasses and stunted shrubs of the low tundra of coastal northwestern Alaska, this **Western Sandpiper** *(left)* and its chick are situated only a few inches above the frozen ground, or permafrost, and barely above the water table. The cover and warmth a sandpiper parent provides are vital to the growth and development of the nestling, which must take place quickly in the short arctic summer. After hatching, Western Sandpiper chicks are precocial; they can walk and feed themselves almost immediately. By mid-July, the adults have departed the tundra, leaving the young to develop their flying skills in preparation for their long autumn migration.

As the tundra landscape of northern Manitoba changes from snowy white to springtime green, the plumage of the **Willow Ptarmigan** *(right)* changes, too, to better blend in with the bird's environment. Both male and female ptarmigan lose their pure-white plumage as winter gives way to spring. The females become more cryptic to better hide while on their nests amidst shrubby vegetation. The ptarmigan's downy feathers, which cover even its feet, serve another purpose, offering superb insulation against the arctic cold.

Although it is brightly colored for a shorebird, the plumage of the **Ruddy Turnstone** *(right)* does not seem to prevent the bird from nesting successfully on the open arctic tundra. The rusty back and vivid harlequin markings would appear to be a disadvantage for birds nesting on the ground. To compensate, the turnstone must be ever alert to imminent danger. With its head raised, this turnstone, photographed in Nome near the southern terminus of its nesting range, is poised to flee at the slightest disturbance.

Seeing **Rock Ptarmigan** *(left)* and **Willow Ptarmigan** together is unusual. During the nesting season, Willow Ptarmigan generally inhabit low tundra, while Rock Ptarmigan thrive in higher elevations, especially on mountain ridges. The species intermingle only when Rock Ptarmigan migrate to lower elevations in search of food. These four birds have already molted into their white plumage in preparation for a snowy arctic winter. Of course, the white camouflage isn't useful if the ground is without snow cover.

These juvenile **Winter Wrens** await food from their parents. Although not truly an arctic or tundra species, the Winter Wren thrives on the Pribilof Islands off western Alaska, where the habitat is similar to the arctic tundra. The wrens seem to be as equally adapted to tundra-like surroundings as they are to the thickly forested hillsides where birders usually see them. On the Pribilofs, Winter Wrens nest among rocks and short shrubs; in northern hardwood forests, they nest under logs and brush—a good example of a species truly adapted to a wide variety of nesting situations, an unusual trait among birds.

Savannah Sparrows are grass-land-nesting birds adapted to living in open spaces from far northern Alaska and Canada southward to New Mexico. Because the arctic tundra is structurally similar to the grass-land, the sparrows are perfectly at home there, and vast numbers can be found throughout arctic habitat. In fact, in most of North America where there is open grassland or grass-covered tundra, Savannah Sparrows can be found, eating insects during the nesting season and grass and other seeds during the remainder of the year. The bird pictured is singing a high-pitched, insectlike song that varies throughout the species' range.

Perhaps one of the most beautiful gulls, the **Ross's Gull** (*right*) usually has a pinkish tinge to its plumage that comes from oil preened onto its feathers. Experts believe that the crustaceans these birds consume make their preening oil pink; a similar situation occurs with some flamingos. Its delicate color and distinctive head marking make the Ross's Gull a memorable sight for birders when it makes a rare appearance south of its arctic home.

Although it appears that this **Parasitic Jaeger** (*left*) is vocalizing or engaged in display behavior, it is actually trying to catch a mosquito. Jaegers and other tundra nesters must deal with a continuous onslaught of mosquitos during their nesting season. The only respite is a strong wind. Parasitic Jaegers look like gulls, but they make their living as predators of insects, small birds, and mammals. They are agile fliers and can swoop in to steal eggs from waterfowl nests that are left unattended. All jaegers are highly parasitic, especially during the nonbreeding season, which they spend at sea.

With long, tapering wings and pointed tails, **Long-tailed Jaegers** (*right*) cruise the open skies above Alaska's mountainous arctic tundra, scanning for the lemmings that make up the bulk of their diet during the nesting season. So important is the lemming population to the jaeger's nesting success that if the rodents are not present in huge numbers, the birds will nest elsewhere. After the nesting season, the jaeger changes its ways, migrating to the open sea, where it feeds on marine life, often stolen from gulls and other less skillful fliers.

It's clear why the **Dunlin** was formerly called the Red-backed Sand-piper, which might be a better name for the species. The Dunlin's nest is a simple structure built in low-growing shrubs or tundra grasses and often lined with fine leaves of Lapland rosebay or similar vegetation. The Dunlin's eggs are mottled to blend in with the leaves so that aerial predators, such as ravens, gulls, and jaegers, cannot spot them when the parents are off the nest, which occurs when they exchange incubation duties or perform distraction displays.

The rich chestnut coloration of the breeding **Short-billed Dowitcher** stands out against the gray of an arctic boulder. Rocks serve an important purpose for birds that live on the tundra. They offer resting places and lookout perches in an environment that lacks tall vegetation. They also offer something of a safe haven from predators, even if they are only a few inches above the ground.

Sitting motionless on a nest, this male **Stilt Sandpiper** is well camouflaged against a backdrop of tundra grasses, dwarf shrubs, and low vegetation. Male stilts usually incubate in the daytime; females take over at night, although during the arctic summer it is sometimes difficult to differentiate between night and day. As soon as the eggs hatch, female stilts abandon their chicks; the male abrogates responsibility two weeks later. Young stilts must mature quickly: they are completely on their own come July, when the adults leave for South America. The young depart separately a few weeks after.

During migration and throughout the nonbreeding season, **Rock Sandpipers** live up to their name. They are most likely to be seen on rocky or gravel coastlines, from Alaska to northern California, feeding on the small crustaceans and other marine life they find in the nooks and crannies of the intertidal zone. During the nesting season, like many other shorebirds, Rock Sandpipers forsake the unvegetated ocean coastline for the short grass, moss, and stunted shrubs of the arctic tundra.

24

Conspicuously plumed male **Lapland Longspurs** often find the tallest objects, which are usually less than a foot high, to use as sentinel perches from which to scan their territory for intruding males and predators. Because they nest on the ground, within easy reach of mammalian enemies, Lapland Longspurs conceal their nests in arctic grass and moss, weaving a cup out of pliable vegetation. Birds of temperate grasslands construct similar nests for the same reason. Longspur nests have another requirement, however. The grass lining must protect eggs from bitter arctic winds and breeding-season snowstorms—occurrences that rarely affect birds of warmer climes.

Hudsonian Godwits, like virtually all shorebirds, are ground nesters and birds of wide-open spaces, so scenes like this one are rare. Godwits nest in the arctic tundra and southward into the taiga, not far from the northern terminus of trees; their nests are usually covered by tundra grasses, making them almost impossible to find. This bird may have been escaping a swarm of early-summer mosquitos or trying to get a good view of the surrounding terrain. Godwits often nest near trees, and this bird may have been only a short distance from its nest, which would most likely be in a dry spot near water.

A rocky outcropping on the Pribilof Islands off the coast of Alaska serves a dual purpose for a **Snow Bunting.** It offers a convenient perch and launching location for low-level aerial displays, which include both flight and song. It also provides an excellent site for a nest, tucked among the rocks away from wind and rain. Young buntings like the one at left stay near the nest, where they beg for food. Unlike adult males, they are rather inconspicuous as they sit on the rocks, surrounded by stunted shrubs and lichens. Within weeks, they will join hundreds of other Snow Buntings in their migration southward.

Young **Canada Geese** are precocious and will begin to feed on insects almost immediately after they can walk. They instinctively peck at nearby bugs and any other small object that moves; they are able to feed themselves soon after hatching. Many populations of arctic Canada Geese nest on islands in the Canadian tundra, where they are relatively safe from mammalian predators. The chicks are still vulnerable to aerial attacks, however, until they learn to fly.

At home in the bleak, rock-strewn expanses of the high arctic, **Northern Wheatears** nest across the tundra of most of the western and eastern hemispheres. In Europe and parts of Asia, they nest far into the temperate zone. In North America, however, they never nest south of the high arctic. The North American birds' distribution might be limited by their migration pattern. Wheatears that breed in Alaska and western Canada migrate westward into Asia for the winter. Those that breed in eastern Canada and Greenland migrate to the southeast into Europe and Africa. Nesting farther south in the western hemisphere would force these birds to migrate longer distances over water, which might be impossible for this species.

Forest and Field

THE WORLD'S FORESTS HARBOR SOME OF THE RICHEST AND MOST DIVERSE ASSEMBLAGES OF BIRDS.
A hundred acres of forest in New England can offer shelter and sustenance to dozens of species:
songbirds, hawks, owls, and others. So many birds thrive in forested areas because of the vertical
diversity of habitats; birds can nest and feed from the ground all the way up to the tops of the trees.
For example, Ovenbirds nest on the forest floor and forage in the lower parts of the forest even as
kinglets nest and forage higher up. As well, a variety of trees satisfies a variety of appetites. Some
birds feast on insect larvae in the needles of spruce trees while others find prey on the undersides
of maple or oak leaves. Birds of the forest feed throughout the vertical column of vegetation, and
each species is adapted to a particular set of habitat conditions. In fact, there are so many niches
and food sources in the forest to exploit that descriptions of forest foraging habits and habitats
alone could fill several good-sized books.

Some of the world's most colorful birds live in the forest. Warblers, with their brilliant yellows
and golds, flit through the canopy; brightly colored tanagers forage in the middle layers; thrushes,
with their muted browns and rust colors, stalk the forest floor. They employ a variety of methods
to catch their food. Some birds walk along the ground, probing for insects in leaf litter. Others
"hawk" insects, catching them on the wing. Still others work the crevices of tree trunks and branches
in search of a meal.

Throughout the years, suburban development and farmland creation have greatly affected a large
portion of the forest in North America. Cleared forests mean the loss of trees but create what are
called "edge" habitats: wooded lands that border clearings. This fragmentation of the forest threatens birds that rely on large, unbroken tracts of woods while favoring species that prefer more open
areas. The latter include backyard visitors like the Northern Cardinal and Common Yellowthroat.
Where they once were rare, edge species are now often quite common. And what was once a vast,
mature forest has now become a mosaic of woodland and field habitats, hurting some bird populations while helping others.

A **Barn Owl** perched in the open during daylight, like this one, is likely to have been disturbed from a secluded perch—probably by a flock of mobbing crows. Or perhaps it's just hunting for a last snack at dawn. During the day, these birds normally perch in old barns and derelict structures, or in thick vegetation or the cavity of a tree, where they will be safe and undisturbed. Barn Owls usually leave their daytime roosts only at night, when they forage over marshes, fields, lawns, and city streets.

Few birds outside of the tropics are as colorful as the male **Painted Bunting.** Its electric colors strongly suggest neotropical origins, and, indeed, the bird does nest in the southern United States and northern Mexico. This bunting perches in a mesquite thicket in southern Texas on its way north after a winter in Mexico. Such thickets have disappeared in much of the brush country of south Texas, requiring migrants like Painted Buntings to rest and feed in unsuitable habitats or move farther north before stopping.

After it "binds," or holds fast, to its prey, this **Northern Goshawk** mantles its meal, as do most other raptors. The outstretched wings and tail serve to balance the hawk while its prey dies as well as protect and conceal its prey from other predators, like other hawks and foxes, while it eats. Although the goshawk will sometimes carry prey to a secure location, it often eats its victim where it is captured. Consuming a large meal like a Ruffed Grouse can take a half hour or more. Goshawks nest in small numbers in the United States and are usually seen after they migrate from forests far to the north or high-elevation forests of the western mountains. This "irruption" occurs when prey is scarce or when goshawk populations are exceptionally large.

The barbed wire fence on which this **Mountain Bluebird** perches tells a great deal about the habitat preference of the species, which is usually found at higher elevations along edges where forests border fields. Like most members of the thrush family, Mountain Bluebirds are primarily insectivorous during the summer months, although they switch to other foods, including fruits, during the colder seasons. This male has just captured a large larva, which it will quickly deliver to its waiting young. Adult bluebirds make thousands of food deliveries to their chicks during the nesting season.

Among the smallest of songbirds, **Golden-crowned Kinglets** weigh only about a quarter of an ounce. Although its nesting habitat is usually in the high-elevation forests of the northern United States and across Canada, this bird can be found in a variety of environments during the rest of the year. Like many forest species, kinglets must use the habitats that are available during migration, which include various kinds of forests and even open fields. This kinglet searches the underside of plants' leaves for insects hiding beneath a field's "canopy." Kinglets also chase flying insects and glean from the bark of trees. The ability to find food in diverse habitats helps these birds migrate through areas where the food supply is uncertain and unpredictable.

Only three inches long and weighing one-seventh of an ounce, hummingbirds seem more like insects than birds. **Anna's Hummingbirds** breed in coastal lowlands of the west coast, building their nests in the crotches of small trees, often in suburban gardens and park thickets. Hummingbird nests are only two to three inches across but are more elaborate than most birds'. Anna's nests are made of leaves and grasses held together with spider silk and lined with feathers and fine plant material. The outside is often covered with lichens. The nest's thick walls insulate the eggs and young to protect them from cooling—particularly dangerous to hummingbirds because they are so tiny.

In the mid-1900s, **Eastern Bluebird** populations suffered enormous declines as a result of pesticide use and the harvesting of dead trees in which they nested. In recent years, however, the most dangerous of pesticides have been outlawed, and a concerted effort to create nest sites by placing nest boxes along the edges of forests and fields has resulted in a marvelous recovery of the species. Nest boxes actually have several advantages over natural cavities. They are cleaned during winter, which eliminates many nest parasites. Also, the entrance hole can be precisely controlled so that interlopers like starlings, which are larger, cannot evict nesting bluebirds. As well, nest boxes are often tended so that the nests of unwanted visitors, like House Sparrows, can be tossed out.

The deep blood-red eyes and slate gray back of this **Sharp-shinned Hawk** identify it as an adult; birds older than two years usually have red eyes. Adult sharpies are more secretive and therefore less often observed in the wild than are first-year birds. This adult paused during migration to scan the horizon for prey. The bird is alert for good reason: although they are predators, Sharp-shinned Hawks are one of the smallest raptors and are not infrequently captured and eaten by larger raptors, including Cooper's Hawks and Peregrine Falcons.

Like many raptors, **Cooper's Hawks** employ a mixed strategy for catching prey. Most of the time, the bird uses a sit-and-wait tactic. By perching quietly, it won't be noticed by prey like doves or mice, which can be surprised at close range. Usually the hawk perches at the edge of a field, but at times it will wait in the open. Cooper's Hawks also use a cruise-hunting strategy, flying low along forest edges, over brushy fields, or through forests, searching for unsuspecting prey. In-flight hunting helps the hawk get the jump on its victim as it tries to flee. The hawk's long legs and toes are adaptations for catching prey in thick brush.

Birders rarely get a good look at **Northern Saw-whet Owls.** Although thousands of these birds migrate through the northern United States and southern Canada each year, only a handful are ever detected. The owl's favorite daytime roosts include thick conifers, holly trees, and tangles of Japanese honeysuckle or other vines, in which they are all but invisible. Even when a human comes within a few feet of a saw-whet, it does not move. In Manhattan's Central Park, saw-whet owls spend the winter in quiet harmony with thousands of walkers, joggers, and cyclists. At dusk, they leave the safety of their daytime roosts to seek mice and small birds.

To most birders, **White-throated Sparrows** are birds of winter. When snow cover is deep, white-throats are among the most common of feeder birds, picking among leaves and scratching at the ground to uncover seeds and other morsels. They are at home in the snow and ice as far north as southern Canada and are tolerant of brutal cold as long as they are well fed. Backyards are a long way from the northern and high-elevation forests where these birds nest, but come autumn, white-throats readily invade yards and fields that have thick brush nearby: conditions are much less severe there than they are in the forest. Because of the abundance of backyard feeders, White-throated Sparrows need not migrate as far south as they did a century ago.

The fruit-loving **Hermit Thrush** is a sucker for pokeberry, American holly, viburnum, multiflora rose, and most other species of fruiting plants. Although it's unusual to see Hermit Thrushes outside of the forest, during migration the lure of a bounty of fruit is often more than the bird can resist. After an exhausting night on the wing, migrants are often so hungry they forsake their preferred forest habitats to forage in the open. Unlike other thrushes, Hermit Thrushes rarely migrate to the tropics. Instead, after nesting in northeastern forests, they winter as far north as southern New England and Ohio. The reason this species stays so far north while closely related Veery, Swainson's, and Bicknell's thrushes go to the tropics remains a mystery; natural selection seems to have made the Hermit Thrush more tolerant of brutal weather and better able to survive on fruit during the winter.

The sweet song of the **Baltimore Oriole** is a sure sign of spring. At about the same time these birds return from the tropics, apple, pear, and other fruit trees are in full bloom. Although orioles are primarily insectivorous in spring and summer and frugivorous during autumn and winter, they rarely pass up the chance to feed on the nectar of flowers, or even at hummingbird feeders. Nectar provides an energy-rich alternative to insects for these birds. This migrant male is foraging in May on insects attracted to the sweet flowers of a beach plum in dunes along the Atlantic coast.

The **Northern Cardinal** is slowly spreading northward, extending its range into the northern United States and southern Canada. A forest edge and brush species, this familiar bird loves tangles and thickets with the occasional tall tree or hedgerow; it often lives near homes, gardens, and roadsides. This female cardinal perches on a Japanese bittersweet vine, an alien plant that has become entrenched in many parts of the United States; cardinals relish the vine's bittersweet berries. Other introduced plants, such as Japanese honeysuckle, multiflora rose, Russian olive, and privet, have helped promote the northern extension of cardinals by providing sustenance during winter. As well, backyard feeders provide another source of food in areas where this and other species could not naturally survive. Before humans altered the forests of the Northeast, the habitat was mostly unsuitable for cardinals, especially in winter.

The brilliant red plumage of this male **Scarlet Tanager** stands out against the green forests of pine, oak, and maple in which it nests. It has no hope of blending into the background. Like Painted Buntings, tanagers look like tropical birds. The tanager family consists of more than a hundred tropical species—most sport amazing plumage colors, with some looking downright unnatural. In autumn, male Scarlet Tanagers lose their red plumage and become a subtle warm green.

The ability of the **Yellow Warbler** to use a variety of habitats for nesting helps explain why it is among the most common of all warblers. Yellow Warblers nest in young forests, forest edges, hedgerows in farm fields, orchards, willow groves along water, and even gardens with some trees and brush. While many warblers that nest in interior forests have declined in numbers, the species as a whole seems to be expanding as forests are fragmented and old fields undergo succession.

Common Yellowthroats are another species that has benefited as forests have become fragmented and old farms revert to brush and thickets. They nest in the thick understory of forests, along forest edges, and in hedgerows; they are likely to be found near human habitation. Birders often hear the raspy calls of these tiny warblers before they see the bird. Skulking low in the brush, yellowthroats are usually overlooked unless they scold intruders or move to an exposed perch to examine a pishing birder. Even then they seldom stay in view for long. Birders must be quick with their binoculars or they will miss the show.

The blooms of a flowering beach plum act as magnets for insects, which in turn attract a **Northern Parula.** It's not unusual to see the bills of songbirds covered with pollen as they feast on insects hidden inside the flowers. Although it looks like the birds are eating the pollen, they only consume it accidentally as they gorge on protein-rich bugs. Beach plums generally grow along seashore dunes—not the usual nesting and foraging habitat of the Northern Parula or most other warblers. Parulas most often live high in a mature canopy of oak and other deciduous trees, where they glean insects off leaves and bark. They favor high perches from which to sing, making them difficult to observe. After a long migration over the ocean, this parula forages close to the ground, a rare treat for a birder.

Although **Tree Swallows** *(left and above)* prefer to perch on dead tree snags, where they can be alone as they rest or watch for insects, they sometimes must use whatever perches are available. As hundreds of thousands or even millions of these swallows pass through coastal areas during migration, they often have only the beach or sand dunes on which to perch—a comfortable place on a chilly afternoon when the sand is still warm. Migrating Tree Swallows will also rest on asphalt parking lots and highways to take advantage of the warmth of the road surface, which at times puts them in harm's way. Flocks resting in cool weather usually face away from the wind to reduce heat loss.

Purple Martins *(below)*, like other swallows, are particularly social during migration, often perching so close together that they touch each other. Because martins come north earlier than most insectivorous birds, they encounter cool temperatures and often a paucity of flying insects. A cold spell sometimes causes many of the earliest migrants to starve. To conserve energy during adverse conditions, martins often roost together to keep their bodies from cooling. Male Purple Martins arrive at their nesting grounds a few days to more than a week before the females, who then choose males with the best-looking nest sites. Although the evolutionary mechanism that drives this differential migration is not completely understood, most scientists believe that competition among males for nest sites and female choice of mates are the driving forces.

Ten days after hatching, a **Florida Scrub-Jay** is more than halfway to fledging. These jays are "anting," a behavior that involves rubbing ants into their feathers as they preen. Secretions from the ants are thought to act as an insect repellent. Because scrub-jays are social and have extended families present at the nest, the structure itself needs to be strong enough to support a number of birds. Scrub-jays are cooperative breeders, with nonparents, usually birds from the previous year's clutch waiting for a chance to nest, helping to raise the young by providing food and guarding against predators. Their presence increases the chance of nesting success. Scrub-jay families often nest in the same area year after year, so nests are sometimes reused, growing larger and heavier as they are rebuilt. In central Florida, where these scrub-jays were photographed, forest-scrub habitats are rapidly disappearing to development. The bird is now listed in Florida as a "species of concern."

Gram for gram, the **Black-capped Chickadee** may be the toughest bird in North America. At northern latitudes, chickadees survive more than four months of deep snow, subzero temperatures, and brutal winds. They survive, in part, by virtue of the availability of food provided by feeders and, in part, by roosting in cavities of trees during long winter nights. Cavities offer a microclimate protected from the wind and insulated against the cold.

A **Tufted Titmouse** sits at the top of a sumac tree, perhaps contemplating the flavor of the dried fruit it is about to consume. Though not terribly frugivorous, titmice can eat a variety of foods, which is virtually required for year-round residency in northern latitudes. Several species of sumac are an important autumn and winter food for titmice. They also eat insects, seeds, even spiders—whatever is available. Expanding suburbia, which has created numerous edge habitats and brought with it increasing numbers of backyard bird-feeders, has helped the titmouse extend its range northward.

The nasal *yank, yank* of the **White-breasted Nuthatch** is a familiar sound in oak and maple forests of the eastern United States and Canada. This gymnast resembles a tiny woodpecker as it works its way up and down the trunks of trees, gleaning insects from crevices as it hangs upside-down or assumes other unlikely postures. To feed in this way, nuthatches have powerful feet that help them defy gravity as they work the undersides of branches and hanging bark. The nuthatch's woodpeckerlike bill allows it to excavate bark and rotten wood as it searches for food.

Marsh, Lake, and River

FRESHWATER, WHETHER SHALLOW OR DEEP, STILL OR RUNNING, PRESENTS A SUITE OF ENVIRONMENTAL situations with which birds must contend. Birds that nest or feed in wetland or habitats with water have a larger and more diverse array of behaviors and adaptations than do birds that inhabit terrestrial situations. The result is that many wetland and aquatic birds look and act much differently from birds of other habitats.

Birds of the inland waters have a host of adaptations for dealing with their unique environment. For feeding alone, they possess a variety of structural adaptations. Some birds have long legs so they can wade into the water while they search for food. Some have oily plumage or feathers that trap air to help them shed water or stay afloat. Others have webbed or partially webbed feet for swimming, or long toes for walking on soft mud or lily pads. Aerial foragers have strong flight muscles and aerodynamically streamlined bodies to stay aloft while scanning for prey.

The birds in this chapter are found along rivers, marshes, streams, lakes, and other freshwater or brackish aquatic environments. Like the species in other chapters, they provide a diverse view of how birds make a living in and near their unique habitats.

Wetlands and, to a lesser extent, aquatic habitats have been eliminated or modified by filling, ditching, dredging, straightening, channeling, and other activities for more than a century. Over the years, vast areas of marsh, swamp, and stream and river edge have disappeared. Instead of natural wetlands or riparian areas, in many parts of North America we now have houses, roads, farms, shopping centers, and industrial parks. The result has been a dramatic decline of many bird species that use freshwater habitats.

Recently hatched **Black-crowned Night-Herons** find safety amidst hundreds of other heron, egret, and ibis nests. The colonies are usually located in small forests and brushy patches on islands in rivers and lakes, where the birds are safe from predators and undisturbed by humans. These herons were photographed on the Isle of Meadows in the Arthur Kill, an industrial river that separates New Jersey from Staten Island. In the shadow of an enormous landfill, this small forested island supports more than six hundred nesting pairs of herons, egrets, and ibis. Night-heron nests, situated in trees sometimes only a few feet off the ground, are so fragile that it is sometimes possible to see the eggs through the bottom. The nest is unlined, and the eggs sit precariously on top of a few twigs. A thin overhead canopy of leaves protects young herons from the hot sun. Within two weeks, these chicks will outgrow their nest and perch on nearby branches until they are old enough to fly.

Unlike most peeps, **Pectoral Sandpipers** seldom frequent wide-open tidal flats during migration. Instead, they prefer marsh edges or the edges of wet meadows. This immature pectoral was photographed in a brackish, wet meadow of grasses and reeds, where it was foraging. Moving slowly along the grassy edge of shallow water, the bird finds small aquatic insects or terrestrial insects in the water or on the grass. As it forages, the bird remains inconspicuous so it won't attract the attention of falcons and other predators.

There are many ways to catch a fish. Like terns, **Belted Kingfishers** dive into the water headfirst, but they most often do so from a perch, sometimes up to thirty feet high: a tree branch, telephone pole, overhead wire, dock piling—anything that offers a good view of the water. To grab fish underwater, kingfishers use their large, scissorlike bills. Fish up to three inches long are swallowed whole. The kingfisher at left is not yawning; it's opening its mouth to help it gulp down a large meal. The nesting habits of Belted Kingfishers are unorthodox. They dig a burrow—often three feet deep—in a steep bank along rivers, streams, and lakes. The eggs are laid at the bottom of the burrow, and the young fledge about forty-seven days later. The steep banks keep raccoons and other climbing predators with a taste for kingfisher eggs away from the nests.

To see a bird with a seven-foot wingspan engaged in aerobatic displays is nothing short of breathtaking. The adult **Bald Eagle** in this sequence was photographed near Homer, Alaska, as it tried to catch a nearly dead salmon. In the first picture *(opposite page)*, the bird begins its rapid descent by turning onto its side, with feet, wings, and tail outstretched, then almost stalling before rolling upside-down. These quick movements position the bird to make a wicked dive. In the last photo the bird begins to accelerate toward the water seventy feet below. Wings no longer outstretched, the eagle quickly gains speed. Such maneuvers are an effective way to capture prey—usually ducks or fish—or outrace another eagle to a meal. Rarely seen by human observers, aerial displays are nonetheless common wherever there are rich sources of food.

Although this **Snowy Egret** is pictured in the type of open habitat near water where the species likes to forage, this bird is not searching for food. Instead, it is being as conspicuous as possible, strutting on a mudflat so that others of its species can see it clearly. With long feathers standing erect on its head, back, and breast, this egret is at the pinnacle of its breeding plumage stage, and it's doing its best to show that it is ready to mate. To complete its display, it will point its beak skyward or fly in a stereotypical fashion. Such displays are common before and during the nesting season: May and June in the northeastern United States. Shortly thereafter, the luxurious plumes molt, not to return until the next nesting season.

Least Bitterns (*above*) are secretive animals, almost invisible within their fresh and brackish marsh habitats. They move at a snail's pace, rarely fly, and almost never leave the safety of tall grasses. They do not want to be seen. They live in the shadow of phragmites, cattail, and other vegetation, foraging from perches just above the water line. They creep about, moving one foot at a time, from perch to perch, looking for small fish, crustaceans, and other invertebrates. Like some other birds that nest in marshes, bitterns have experienced steep population declines where this habitat has been reduced or eliminated.

It doesn't take a large marsh to support a **Green Heron** (*left*). The bird's small size and rather secretive hunting techniques permit it to use a diversity of tiny ponds and marshes throughout its range. It's often present but unseen, hunting quietly at the edge of the vegetation, clinging to the low-hanging branches of trees or cattails, waiting for fish, frogs, or large insects to come within reach. The tall grasses of the Everglades, where this bird was photographed, support a large Green Heron population that usually goes unnoticed by those who are passing through.

Paddling furiously with legs set far back on its body—an adaptation for swimming underwater and chasing fast-moving prey—a **Western Grebe** snatches and bolts a smelt before a gull or other parasitic bird takes the fish away. Western Grebes flock to tidal pools, narrow passages in rivers and streams, or upwelling areas in the ocean that attract and hold large numbers of baitfish and the predators that feed on them. While miles of ocean and bay may be devoid of grebes and other predators, small areas where the fishing is good are usually packed with birds.

The **Great Blue Heron,** shown here with days-old hatchlings, is a colonial nester, often nesting among hundreds of others of its species, usually in trees adjacent to water. Occasionally, it nests in suburban settings. The great blue does not tolerate disturbance very well, but if water surrounds its nesting area, forming a protective barrier between it and intruders, nesting near human activity may occur. In fact, it appears that herons and egrets may be adapting to nest nearer human populations. As long as their nests are not plundered by pets and other predators that are sustained by human-provided food sources, Great Blue Herons are likely to thrive.

American Bitterns believe they are invisible if they lift their beaks skyward. Their streaked plumage provides a nearly perfect camouflage when they stand in tall marsh vegetation like cattail, bulrush, rice, or cordgrass. When the bittern points its head upward, the streaks on the bird's neck parallel the grasses, making the bird very difficult to see. This behavior protects the bittern from predators such as Golden Eagles. Freshwater marshes in the northern forests are the preferred nesting, foraging, and hiding places of American Bitterns. As these habitats have been filled and drained, the species has experienced a major population decline over much of its range. Northern forest populations remain intact, but the bird is virtually gone in much of the Northeast and Midwest. Protection of freshwater nesting marsh is crucial to the survival of the species.

59

A duck perched in a tree is a bizarre sight. But the **Black-bellied Whistling-Duck** is arboreal and is as likely to be seen in a tree as in the water. Whistling-duck populations are stable even though the ebony trees they favor for nesting are all but gone along the Rio Grande River of south Texas, an important habitat. This bird, perched in a willow tree, is giving the high-pitched whistling vocalization that characterizes the species. The bird has become a familiar visitor along the Gulf coast from south Texas to Florida.

While it may seem that this **Cinnamon Teal** is simply stretching its wings, it is actually displaying for a prospective mate. The wing stretch is part of a stereotyped display common to many waterfowl. Like Red-winged Blackbirds and Northern Shovelers, male teal flash their wing patch, or speculum, for nearby ducks to see. This bird was wintering in Newport Back Bay in southern California. In late winter or very early spring, it will move with its mate to a nesting site inland. The displays of these and other ducks on the wintering grounds help reinforce pair bonds that remain throughout the year, or even throughout the birds' lives.

The low profile of a **Common Loon** is a familiar sight on the lakes of North America's northern forests. The striking bird nests along undeveloped shorelines of cold-water lakes surrounded by deep woods. As long as there are plenty of fish and privacy, loons usually thrive. The acidification of northern lakes caused by acid rain, however, and the development of lakeshores for vacation homes have driven loons from many places where they once were common.

In the winter, waterfowl such as **Northern Pintail** spend much of their time loafing. The relaxed position of this pintail's neck shows that it is comfortable and not alert. The stretching wing reveals the bird's striking green speculum. Late in the winter, thousands of pintails gather in safe places to wait for spring. Their preferred winter habitat is fresh or tidal marshland dominated by grasses. While there, the birds rest, establish or reinforce pair bonds, feed, and put on fat for migration. Seeds of wetlands plants and cultivated cereal-grain crops are the primary sources of food: wild and cultivated rice, barley, bulrush, and pondweed. Refuges like Bosque del Apache in New Mexico, where this photo was taken, are important because they provide protected areas for waterfowl to rest and eat. Because some pintails undertake spring migration flights of more than two thousand miles, the importance of such resting and feeding sites cannot be overstated.

In winter during the 1930s, birders from nearby states journeyed to New Jersey's Delaware Bay shore to see a few dozen **Snow Geese:** the small flock on the salt marshes behind the town of Fortescue was quite a novelty. It constituted most of the winter population of the species in much of the Northeast at that time. Today, the south Jersey Snow Goose population numbers nearly a quarter of a million. The birds fill the skies of bayshore and coastal marshes. The flapping wings of thousands of birds may delight onlookers, but the geese have wreaked havoc on the marshes as well as their tundra nesting habitat. Because they feed on the part of the vegetation that is belowground, they must tear their food from the soil before they eat it. Called "eat-outs" by wildlife biologists, the barren areas left by thousands of feeding geese are of little use to most wildlife. The species is now a contentious species to manage. Efforts to reduce their populations have not been successful.

With wings held low, the **Red-winged Blackbird** *(above)* shows off its bright red epaulets to other black-birds. Such behavior is a territorial advertisement that tells other males to stay away. Red-wings are one of the most vocal and colorful birds of fresh and brackish marshes. On sunny April days across the country, millions of red-wings find perches above the vegetation, give their distinctive *conk-a-ree* song, and display their wing patches. When red-wings sing, they usually drown out the other birds that are singing in the marsh. The red epaulets are usually kept hidden, but in the flock at right the epaulets are obvious. Red-wings have the ability to cover their red epaulets by sliding other feathers over them. Hiding the markings from other red-wings avoids agonistic behavior, insuring harmony within the flock. Occasion-ally, the epaulets are flashed during the nonbreeding season to secure a preferred feeding spot and keep other red-wings at a distance.

Anhingas *(right)* build rather large nests, often in colonies with other Anhingas or wading birds. They also use old nests of egrets and herons as a foundation upon which to build. Sturdy Anhinga nests are used year after year, with new sticks, leaves, and marsh grasses added at the beginning of the nesting season. Once the eggs hatch, after about twenty-eight days of incubation, Anhingas feed their young regurgitated fish. By the end of the nesting season, an Anhinga colony can be an unpleasant place to visit, as fish, regurgitated bits of flesh, feces, and dead chicks rot in the subtropical sun.

This **American White Pelican** appears to be out of control, but it's actually trying to land and grab fish parts simultaneously. Photographed at a dock as anglers cleaned their catches, this pelican was one of several vying for scraps. It saw other birds feeding and immediately flew to the action. As it arrived, it used its wings as breaks and waterskied into its landing on its webbed feet. This posture can be used as an aggressive display in competitive situations. The fast approach with wings outstretched and mouth agape threatens other birds away from food.

A nest woven and suspended in cattails or other marsh grasses is easily recognizable as that of a **Marsh Wren.** The nest, an intricately woven structure, is usually suspended only a short distance above the marsh. About the size of a softball, the nest is so well constructed that it rarely falls. It provides protection from rain and wind needed to keep young and eggs that weigh only a gram or two warm. Marsh wrens often construct more than a dozen nests within their territory. Polygynous male wrens use the extra nests to attract more than one mate, or perhaps to fool predators or competitors. The construction of so many nests undoubtedly requires an enormous amount of energy, but the benefits of doing so seem to outweigh the drawbacks.

Only a few species of ducks make their living in fast-running streams and rivers. **Common Mergansers** are at home in rapid water, although they also inhabit freshwater lakes and salt or brackish water in much of North America. Catching fish in fast-moving water can't be easy, but mergansers, built somewhat like small loons, are quick and agile swimmers. Like loons, their legs are set far back on their bodies to streamline them and propel them through the water. They often fish in groups, sometimes swimming into the current until they see their prey. The merganser pictured is a female gorging on small eels in a cold salmon stream in Alaska.

Male and female **Wood Ducks** could hardly have more different plumages, with the male (like most ducks) being more ornate and colorful. Wood Ducks frequent ponds, streams, and other calm waters. Although they often forage on land during autumn and winter, the remainder of the year they feed in aquatic situations. Aggressive displays, like the one used by the female at right, keep other woodies away from favorite feeding spots. Lowering the head to the water, opening the mouth, and moving toward another member of the species usually drives competitors off. Such behavior may also function as what is called incitement—females attempting to incite their mates to attack nearby males, which helps establish or reinforce the pair bond prior to copulation and nesting.

The characteristic bobbing tail of the **Spotted Sandpiper** permits quick identification. In Maine, the bird is called "teeter-ass" (pronounced *teeter-ahhss*) because of its unique behavior. Its preferred habitat is also unique. Instead of the wide-open spaces most shorebirds frequent, spotties are found along narrow strips of shoreline: riverbanks, lakeshores, streams, ponds, and bays. The logs, rotting vegetation, and gravel along such shorelines harbor crustaceans and other small animals, like the insect in this bird's bill, upon which the sandpiper feasts. The sex life of the Spotted Sandpiper is different from most birds. Spotties are polyandrous: one female will often mate with two or three males. After laying eggs in one nest, the female leaves the male in charge of brooding and caring for the young. She finds another male and lays another clutch. The nutrient requirement to produce two or three sets of eggs is enormous, so females must feed constantly. This polyandrous strategy works only where prey is superabundant during nesting season. On islands in the lakes of northern Minnesota, enormous hatches of mayflies and other insects in June create an ideal situation for polyandry.

A flock of **Canvasbacks** makes a rapid and steep descent at dawn to feed in a channel on Long Island. Note that the wings of the birds are bowed downward, below the horizontal, and that the birds' feet are extended and fully spread. Both their feet and their wings act as airfoils as the Canvasbacks decelerate into a landing. Within the flock, several of the birds rock from side to side, a result of one wing stalling or encountering turbulence from another bird as they land. The result of a quick jostling is an immediate adjustment and a continued descent. Ducks make a more rapid descent than do land birds; their landings sometimes look like crashes.

Roseate Spoonbills feed by sweeping their enormous paddlelike bills through the shallow water, catching small organisms in a filter similar to a whale's baleen. Spoonbills often preen by rapidly flapping their wings to dislodge detritus, insects, and other debris from between their feathers. After a quick bout of preening, the birds resume feeding. Roseate Spoonbills frequent quiet lagoons and intertidal shallows along the Gulf of Mexico. Here they find the small prey—shrimp and fish—they need to survive.

Refuges like Bosque del Apache serve as transportation terminals for many species of birds; **Sandhill Cranes** *(above)* are frequent visitors. The refuge provides some foraging habitat for the cranes, namely freshwater marsh, grassy areas, and the edges of open water, but not enough for the huge numbers of birds that gather there during migration and over the winter. At dawn, thousands of Sandhill Cranes, mixed with larger numbers of Snow Geese, arise from nighttime roosts within the refuge and fly out into nearby agricultural fields to gorge on unharvested grain, insects, and other small animals.

Although **Purple Gallinules** *(left)* can swim, they are more comfortable walking on the water. Lily pads and other vegetation form floating platforms across which gallinules stalk in search of food. The floating leaves offer partial support; the gallinule's large feet do the rest, spreading the bird's weight over a large surface area so the animal doesn't sink too quickly. Moving across lily pads, the gallinule looks for flowers, seeds, insects, snails, and small vertebrates. The bird makes its home in marshes and lakes with large expanses of dense emergent vegetation, which harbor food and offer shelter from predators, especially alligators.

Amidst cattail and wild-rice marshes across the Midwest and the Great Plains, the brilliant coloring of male **Yellow-headed Blackbirds** makes them readily visible to birders. Such cattails sometimes tower seven feet above the water, but this adult male seems comfortable on its perch, even as the stalk bends in a strong wind. Nesting in cattails in such habitats requires that the large nest be tightly woven with many blades of marsh grass. To advertise its territory, male blackbirds fly above the vegetation with heads held high so all nearby blackbirds can see the yellow signal. Before and after the nesting season, blackbirds, including the yellow-head, gather in large flocks clearly identifiable at a distance.

For a bird the size of a **Great Egret** to land in a small tree, special aerodynamic maneuvers must be called upon. To slow itself upon approach, the bird spreads its wings fully, opens all its primary feathers to the max, extends the alula feathers on its wrists, spreads its tail, and extends its legs downward to increase drag. All these behaviors prevent the bird from stalling in midair and crashing. The aggressive calling and erect head feathers of this egret signal its identity as the owner of a small territory within the heronry.

Entering a colony of herons, egrets, and ibis during the nesting season can be an assault on the senses. Hundreds of birds perch in the trees and fly overhead. Malodorous emanations from decaying food and feces can make even the veteran researcher gag. A constant cacophony prevails. Adults birds are squabbling; the young are begging—loudly and continuously. Sitting on a scrubby tree at the edge of the colony, this juvenile **White Ibis** cackled and called until one of its parents came to feed it. As soon as the chick swallowed its snack, it started to beg all over again.

Desert, Scrub, and Prairie

Vast expanses of horizon and spectacular panoramic views are the norm for most desert, prairie, and, to a lesser extent, scrubland environments. With few trees or tall shrubs to break the horizon, these environments cover vast expanses of western North America, especially in the Midwest, Southwest, Great Plains, and Great Basin. They are primarily two-dimensional worlds, broken only by waterways, potholes, and occasional rivers and hills.

The vegetation of desert, scrub, and prairie is adapted to dry conditions. These regions are too dry for most trees. Rainfall is scarce and highly seasonal, usually no more than twenty inches a year, sometimes much less. The different regions reflect varying stages of dryness: deserts are drier than grasslands, and grasslands are usually drier than scrubland. Birds that live in these environments often time their nesting activities to coincide with the emergence of insects, which, for the most part, are seasonally adapted to the presence of rainfall. When the grasses and other vegetation turn green and insects abound, birds can most easily find the energy and nutrients required to produce eggs and feed young.

Bird communities of the desert, scrub, and prairie are generally less diverse and consist of fewer individuals than do communities in forest and other habitats, except, perhaps, the open ocean, over which birds are scattered widely. Those that live there must cope with a number of environmental challenges. Nesting in prairie grassland is primarily on the ground; in desert, it is in sparse, spiny vegetation. In these situations, birds are often vulnerable to predators. The dry conditions severely limit when and how long food is available. For many species that live in the desert, migration is the primary and most effective strategy for dealing with the seasonal scarcity of food. They expend the energy required to fly away from this habitat during the winter months, which sometimes correspond to the driest season, to go to areas where there is more water and food.

More than other quail, **Gambel's Quail** are at home in the desert, where they live year-round. By confining much of their activity to the early morning and late afternoon, the quail avoid moving during the hottest time of the day. The bird's diet is also adapted to desert life; it eats a variety of seeds, leaves, and plant buds—and insects and fruit if available. Because these foods change seasonally, quail must change their diet often. Like many desert birds, Gambel's Quail are usually found near riparian habitats: creeks, rivers, and other moist places in the desert environment. Perched atop a dead mesquite snag, this male advertises its territory in the Sonoran Desert near the outskirts of Tucson.

The brilliant red coloring of a male **Vermilion Flycatcher** looks more tropical than temperate, distinguishing the small bird from virtually all but a very few North American species. The bird nests only as far north as Arizona and New Mexico and well southward into central Mexico—a true tropical species. Nesting habitat includes mesquite thickets, forested areas along streams, brush, and deserts. This bird is getting ready to spring from its perch to capture an insect.

It's not easy to get a good look at a **Montezuma Quail.** Although considered a desert bird, it is most often found in the mountain forests of the Southwest. Adjacent to true desert, these forests, composed of juniper, oak, and pine, are very dry compared to northern forests. In them, an open understory of grass makes for a parkland environment in which Montezuma Quail thrive. Logging and the destruction of the understory by grazing cattle are eliminating such habitat, although restoration programs in some national forests are helping this species reclaim areas in which it once was common.

From a territorial fence post, this male **Lark Sparrow** advertises and watches over its dry-country domain. In the portion of the Rio Grande Valley where this bird nests, such posts are an important part of the grassland and savanna landscape. They become traditional singing and advertising sites, used by generation after generation of Lark Sparrows and other grassland inhabitants. They also serve as observation posts from which to watch for intruders: wandering males looking for a nesting territory or a mate, or birds from adjacent territories seeking better sources of food.

The distinctive bill of the **Curve-billed Thrasher** is testament to its ability to pry insects and spiders out of deep crevices in rocks and spiny vegetation. This thrasher, photographed in southern Arizona, sits at the top of a saguaro cactus advertising its territory. Because desert habitats do not have tall trees or dense, leafy vegetation, visual displays such as this one—perching on top of a tall saguaro—are sufficient to inform other birds in the area that a territory is occupied. It also tells them exactly who the owner is.

Nectar lapped from flowers is the primary food of virtually all hummingbirds. To find nectar, species like the **Broad-billed Hummingbird** must continually search for flowers that are blooming. In the dry semi-deserts and scrub habitats where broad-bills live, the period during which flowers bloom is short. When hummers find a rich resource, they guard it with vigor, fearlessly diving and buzzing at any and all intruders. Because nectar does not fulfill all of its nutritional requirements, the broad-bill also searches out other foods. The prickly pear cactus hides small insects and spiders that are attracted to its flowers. These invertebrates provide protein, fat, and minerals needed for the hummer to produce eggs and maintain body tissue.

The **Ferruginous Pygmy-Owl** is at home in a variety of habitats throughout Mexico, Arizona, and Texas where scrub and riparian forests offer nesting cavities and prey. Photographed in south Texas, where pygmy-owl populations seem to be declining, this bird perches at the edge of a patch of thorn scrub forest. Most of such brush country along the Mexican border has been eliminated for agriculture. Pygmy-owls are one of the smallest owls, standing only a little more than six inches tall and weighing only about two ounces. They are omnivorous, taking beetles, moths, and small vertebrates like mice. Like other small owls, pygmies usually freeze when humans are nearby and often go unnoticed.

The distinctive wing markings of **White-winged Doves** make them easy to identify in the field. Although these birds are found throughout the desert and dry-brush country that extends along the Mexican border from southern Texas to California, they prefer lush forests along creeks, where feeding opportunities are better than in the desert itself. The doves subsist on a variety of grains, seeds, and cactus fruits and flowers; a favorite food is the inflorescence of yucca or century plant, shown here. Because food is not readily available during some seasons, virtually all White-winged Doves migrate into Mexico for part of the year.

Even though it has a full crop—note the bulging throat—this **Harris's Hawk** continues its single-minded pursuit of prey. The bird is in the final stages of a parachutelike descent into tall grass, where it will attempt to capture a mouse or other prey with its outstretched legs and talons. From this point until the prey is subdued, the action is furious—a quick sequence of grabbing, flapping, jumping, and other gyrations until the prey is secured or escapes. The crop provides a way for raptors to store prey for several hours, until their stomachs empty.

Although the **Burrowing Owl** is catholic in its diet, it only rarely takes reptiles; it is much more likely to eat small mammals and insects. But its diet depends in large part on where it lives. The isolated owl population in the Florida Keys, which frequently does take lizards, has a different diet than the populations that live among prairie dogs or ground squirrels on the western plains. For the most part, the Burrowing Owl hunts during the day and so does not have silent flight. Its primary wing feathers are stiffer and lack the fringed leading edge most nocturnal owls possess. The owl's long flights over open country in pursuit of prey and during migration necessitate stiffer wing feathers.

The plumage of jays and other corvids, such as crows, ravens, and jays, runs the gamut from black to electric blue and green. This **Green Jay** is the most colorful corvid in North America, and like many other brightly colored birds, it has strong tropical affinities. Ranging only a short distance north of the Mexican border, Green Jays are conspicuous residents of bird communities in the scrubby woodlands and riparian forests of Texas' Rio Grande Valley. Like most jays, they are quite social and often live in family groups of four or more individuals.

It seems odd that the jet black **Phainopepla** inhabits the mesquite brushland of the Sonoran Desert, where temperatures regularly climb into the hundreds. Black coloration usually causes heat absorption, but in the case of Phainopeplas and some other black desert birds, the heating occurs only in the feathers and not in the flesh. These unique birds nest once in mesquite and other brush and desert situations early in the year, then move to riparian habitats where vegetation is more lush to nest again. This dramatic and rare change in habitat preference corresponds with changing temperatures and food availability within the nesting season. Food is more available in the desert early in spring and then becomes more available in shaded and moist habitats later.

Desert birds adapt to their harsh and unpredictable habitats in a variety of ways. The bill of the **Pyrrhuloxia** is larger and more decurved than that of the closely related Northern Cardinal, which allows the desert bird to feed more easily on plant matter instead of insects. Breaking open a tough seed or fruit requires a strong bill. The Pyrrhuloxia also ranges over a wide area to locate food in the desert, which is often scarce. In comparison, cardinals living in temperate habitats don't need to range over such a large area.

The **Gila Woodpecker** specializes in making its nests in saguaro and other cacti. It possesses the ability to perch on an extremely thorny plant while excavating a nest. Unlike a cavity in a tree, a newly dug cactus cavity cannot be used until the following season because of the cactus' oozing sap. Does excavating a nest cavity a year before it is needed demonstrate planning? Creating a number of roosting holes and nest sites before they are used greatly increases the odds that at least one will be left alone by other woodpeckers and starlings that usurp gila cavities.

It is not always possible to determine exactly what a bird is communicating to other birds. Displays like this **Crested Caracara's** head-up posture are obviously used to tell nearby birds something, but experts often have to deduce what that something is. In this case, the displaying bird was near a carcass, so the display may be an aggressive signal to warn off others attempting to grab a bit of food. The same posture may also be part of the displays associated with mate selection and pair bonding or the solicitation of sex. Determining what these types of postures mean and how animals communicate is a difficult but rewarding endeavor.

As a year-round resident of the arid Southwest, the **Cactus Wren** is a conspicuous and raucous member of the desert-bird community. Opening their mouths to cool themselves is a way many desert birds cope with extreme heat. As water is evaporated from the inside of the bird's mouth and throat, the blood in nearby capillaries is cooled. Cactus Wrens occasionally forage among the thorns of the saguaro, but they mostly eat their insect diet off the ground.

Brown-crested Flycatchers *(right)* are easy to find. Like most flycatchers, they perch on snags, waiting for winged insects to show themselves. When a grasshopper or other choice morsel zips by, flycatchers dart out, snag the prey in their bills, and consume it on their favorite perch—a method of foraging called "hawking." The same perch is often used for hours, offering ample time to observe flycatcher behavior. Like most flycatchers that depend on flying insects, Brown-crested Flycatchers migrate to the tropics each winter.

Woodpeckers that live in deserts and arid scrub habitats make use of a wider variety of substrates for nesting than do northern forest woodpeckers, which usually use only cavities in trees. The **Ladder-backed Woodpecker** *(below)* uses trees, but it also nests in cacti and, in the case of the bird pictured, a fence post, an invaluable addition to a landscape where trees are absent, such as the Rio Grande Valley.

In some parts of their range, especially the Northeast and parts of the Midwest, **Northern Bobwhite** have undergone enormous population declines. This after the species flourished when heavily forested areas were replaced by old-style, small-scale farms, which created the brushy edge habitats in which bobwhite thrive. Recent suburbanization of small farms has eliminated old and fallow fields and brought new dangers—domestic cats, in particular—to the landscape. Here, a fallow farm field in the Rio Grande Valley covered with wildflowers and other uncultivated plants offers a male bobwhite an abundance of insects, seeds, and shelters.

Seeing a **Common Nighthawk** drinking like this is extremely rare. Although swallows commonly drink on the fly, few other birds do this, and most people have probably never witnessed a nighthawk engage in such behavior. The presence of water during a scorching day in Balmorahea State Park in southwestern Texas lured several Common Nighthawks to drink in the middle of the afternoon. Many birds have unique adaptations to avoid dehydration, including convective cooling and evaporating water from their mouths and air sacs—important adaptations for desert birds, since they can generate body temperatures in excess of 105 degrees during flight.

Ocean and Sea

MOST OCEAN AND SEABIRDS COME TO LAND ONLY TO MATE, LAY EGGS, AND RAISE YOUNG. THEIR LIVES are spent primarily at sea, and some of these species rarely come close enough to land for birders to see them. The truly pelagic, or offshore, seabirds face a number of unique threats to their survival. They must move vast distances, often across hemispheres, to find food. They must ride out horrendous storms without shelter from violent wind and rain. And they must be able to survive with little or no freshwater to drink. Seabirds that spend much of their life near the shore or come ashore more than the truly pelagic species are less adapted to life at sea and frequently have some of the same adaptations as land birds.

The ocean and sea are both rich and poor food sources. Some locations have enormous supplies of plankton and fish for birds to eat while other areas are virtually devoid of life. To survive, seabirds must find the food-rich areas; when they do, they often gather in tremendous numbers. Because these rich patches attract so many birds from far and wide, at any given moment, most of the ocean has no bird life. Some of the food-rich locations produce constantly; others have seasonal patterns during which food, and bird numbers, fluctuate greatly. One month there will be thousands of birds feeding, the next month none.

Most seabirds are powerful fliers, able to move long distances between feeding locations as well as between nesting and wintering areas. They are often characterized by their long, pointed wings, which enable them to fly, in some cases, for thousands of miles. Constant movement is one of the most common features shared by birds at home over the sea. As well, many seabirds are graced with adaptations that allow them to dive from more than a hundred feet above the waves into the water, or dive from the surface of the water several hundred feet below the surface to find their food.

A few of the truly pelagic seabirds are pictured here. Many of the others make their living within a mile or two of the shore, although they occasionally venture well over the horizon. Some, like the scoters and the Harlequin Duck, are not true seabirds, but can be found at the edge of the ocean or a few miles out to sea. They are seaducks, though they nest inland and spend only their nonbreeding life in the ocean. Other species shown here nest along the seacoast on islands, headlands, cliffs, or other remote nearshore locations.

Perched on a cliff more than a hundred feet above the water, a **Crested Auklet** rests a few feet from its nest on an island off the coast of southwestern Alaska. It's hard to fathom how these birds are able to nest on bare rock or dirt in such a cold area. To keep the eggs warm without a nest lining requires diligence and a large amount of energy. It helps that nests are generally protected from the wind by surrounding rocks. Thermal protection is also important in these areas after the eggs hatch, because nestlings cannot regulate their own body temperatures until they are about four or five days old. Like many of the alcids that inhabit arctic and subarctic waters, auklets need an abundant supply of food to provide the energy needed to maintain body temperature.

The bright red inflated throat pouch of this **Magnificent Frigatebird** identifies it as a male performing a courtship display. Soaring over the world's tropical oceans requires a well-adapted array of aerodynamic features. Tropical oceans lack the continuous strong winds and powerful updrafts associated with temperate and arctic waters. With less wind and smaller waves, there are fewer opportunities for birds to soar; birds like the Magnificent Frigatebird are adapted to using weak updrafts. Though they are large, frigatebirds have light wing-loading (the bird's weight in pounds borne by each square foot of wing surface), long wings, and a forked tail that help them stay aloft for much of the day. They can soar to altitudes of a thousand feet above the waves while they search for food and move between foraging locations.

The superb aerodynamic abilities of **Great Frigatebirds** not only permit them to stay aloft for long periods of time without expending much energy, but also facilitate the bird's piratic way of life. Frigatebirds often steal food from other birds that have expended considerable effort to capture a marine goody. With constant harrying, frigatebirds often make gulls, terns, or other birds drop their food, which the pirate can quickly reach and gobble up. Great maneuverability allows frigatebirds to make tight, aerobatic turns and chase smaller birds over the ocean. In areas where frigatebirds are common, if food is not eaten promptly after it is caught, it's an open invitation to what experts call kleptoparasitism: stealing food.

Ocean-facing cliffs annointed liberally with excrement are a sure sign of habitation by large numbers of seabirds. Along the northern Atlantic and Pacific coasts, large colonies of seabirds—murres, auklets, puffins, and the like—make their nesting homes on cliff faces. A single egg on a small ledge wouldn't seem to have much protection from the elements, but it's safe from predators. Adult **Thick-billed Murres** will sometimes incubate an egg for up to three days before being spelled by a mate. The murre hatchling will instinctively stay away from the edge of the cliff until it is ready to fly, so it lives on the ledge for three to four weeks. When it does fly from the ledge, it is one-trial learning. From then on until it breeds, a young murre spends its life mostly at sea.

The **Common Murre** is perfectly comfortable in the cold waters of the Bering Sea and Arctic Ocean. The ability to stay warm while swimming in waters just above freezing is one of the distinguishing features of alcids. An oily plumage with thick down enables these birds to maintain their body temperature even in the coldest waters. This murre was photographed near Homer, Alaska, in March. Although the bird's breeding plumage is different from the winter plumage, the breast and abdomen remain white throughout the year. Experts believe these and other fish-eating birds that swim have white underparts that reflect light so they are less easily detected by their prey. Common Murres are powerful swimmers, often diving several hundred feet to capture fish.

One of the most northerly of alcids, the **Parakeet Auklet** lives mainly in the waters north of the Aleutian Islands. This hardy species survives throughout the year in the Bering Sea and Arctic Ocean on a diet mostly of plankton. Because they nest so far north, little is known about their social behavior. In colonies of alcids, usually situated on cliffs or on steep slopes adjacent to the sea, experts observe constant squabbling over favored positions and nest sites, as well as behavior associated with pair bonding. Once an auklet has young in the nest, most of its time is spent gathering food. Over and over again, for more than a month, the parents fly out to sea, gather plankton in a throat pouch, and return to feed their young. The bird pictured is vocalizing, either in aggression or to beg food from its mate.

Seaducks generally spend most of their lives within sight of shore. **Surf Scoters,** along with related Black Scoters and White-winged Scoters, forage in the shallow nearshore waters of the ocean, wherever mollusks and crustaceans are plentiful and accessible. Called "skunk-heads" by old-time duck hunters, Surf Scoters capture their prey by swimming to the ocean bottom, sometimes in water more than fifteen feet deep, grabbing whatever they can, and returning to the surface. The scoter at right has just surfaced off Bolsa Chica on the southern California coast, grasping a cluster of mussels it wrenched from the rocky bottom. It will most likely crunch the meal into small pieces before swallowing it. Over large mussel beds, hundreds of scoters dive repeatedly. Gulls, attracted to the activity, will attempt to steal whatever food is not carefully guarded. When hundreds of birds converge on a bed, they can have a significant impact on local populations of mollusks and other marine animals. Flying only inches above the water, occasionally skimming the waves, is a behavior characteristic of many waterbirds. The Surf Scoter, like other seaducks, gulls, gannets, pelicans, and cormorants, actually saves energy by using the water's surface to reduce aerodynamic drag. As its wing tips approach the water's surface, or even touch it, the tip vortex—a little swirling donut of air—is shed more easily because it actually "sticks" to the water. When birds fly higher, the tip vortex must be dragged through the air, requiring a greater expenditure of energy.

The sighting of a **Harlequin Duck** along the east coast of the United States generally attracts attention. To the delight of birders, a handful of these brightly colored seaducks winters on the ocean jetties at Barnegat, New Jersey. Harlequins are diving ducks that feed on grass shrimp, small crabs, snails, and other invertebrates in the shallow waters along jetties and rocky shorelines of both coasts. They rarely venture south of New England, though; the rocky shorelines they favor give way to sandy beaches below New Jersey. Man-made jetties, however, resemble rocky beaches and have encouraged some harlequins to winter on more southerly shores.

Atlantic Puffin colonies like the one off Trinity, Newfoundland, are located on small islands just off the coast. From Maine to Greenland, puffins nest in burrows or deep crevices in the sides of hills. When those hillsides are covered with lush grasses and shrubbery, the nests are invisible except at close range. The nests are often lined with vegetation, which keeps the egg off the cold, damp ground. The puffin in the foreground, probably a male, displays by stretching its wings and flapping—part of a courtship display. If the display is successful, it will result in the laying of a single egg, as is the case for many species of puffins, auklets, and murres. Puffins find their food anywhere from a few hundred feet from the colony to many miles away and sometimes dive to depths greater than a hundred feet to capture small fish, squid, and an occasional invertebrate. Atlantic Puffins have the uncanny ability to capture their prey with their bill while at the same time holding tight to previously caught fish. They also can fly many miles with a full beak. To do this with aerodynamic efficiency, the puffin alternates the direction in which the fishes' heads are placed in its bill.

Nesting pairs of **Tufted Puffins** often meet at the nest to exchange incubation duties. During this meeting, they use stereotyped behaviors to make sure the arriving bird is a mate. Here, the bird on the left is leaning forward in an aggressive posture. The arriving bird is more passive, evident from its unbalanced posture. With wings outstretched and flapping, the arriving bird waits until it is accepted by the other. Shortly, the arriving bird will incubate the eggs, allowing the other bird to go off and feed.

Although they are pelagic, **Northern Gannets** are often visible from shore as they soar over the water looking for fish. They remain close to the coast as long as fish are available, and so are a major part of the late autumn procession of migrants down the eastern shore of Canada and the United States. When they see mackerel or menhaden, gannets fold their wings and dive from up to eighty or more feet. They enter the water like a spear, hitting headfirst with wings folded back, often descending several feet below the surface. At a nesting colony at Cape Saint Mary's in Newfoundland, this adult gannet carries a beakful of nesting material—grasses and brown algae. Even amidst hundreds of other colony members, the birds always seem to find their nests.

All seabirds must come ashore to nest. For **Horned Puffins,** during the nesting season, a quarter of their lives is spent in close proximity to the shore. The nest site is usually a few feet back from the cliff face, with the egg and young tucked into a burrow or crevice. The cliff and burrow afford protection from late snowfalls and bitter rain showers common along the northern Pacific coastline. Virtually no predator can rob the egg or young from such nests, which may explain why these birds lay only one egg a year. The relative security of the nesting site insures that parental investment in raising a single young is likely to pay off. So, despite the inhospitable climate and brutal weather these birds must endure, the rate of nesting success on cliffs is high, as long as adequate food is available.

The **Blue-footed Booby** is the tropical equivalent of the Northern Gannet. Like gannets, boobies live much of their lives at sea, catching fish and squid by diving from more than a hundred feet in the air. Occasionally, several boobies will dive at the same time, which may increase their chances of success in capturing fish that scatter to avoid the predators. In some years, especially those associated with El Niño, wholesale reproductive failure occurs in booby colonies. When the waters near the Galapagos Islands grow warm, fish populations plummet, and boobies must fly long distances from their Galapagos nests to find food. If they fail, the birds either don't lay eggs or the young starve. Because boobies are long-lived, their population can usually absorb years of high mortality.

A pair of **Masked Boobies** on the Galapagos Islands has concealed its nest just underneath a clump of tropical vegetation, a shaded location out of the hot sun. Older nestlings are better able to deal with heat stress; although boobies usually lay two eggs, often only one of the young survives. On many occasions, the older of the birds commits what is called siblicide by pushing the younger bird away from the nest. In doing so, it insures that it will get all the food and attention of the parents, while its sibling dies. Laying two eggs may cost the parents energy and nutrients to produce, but it is a kind of insurance policy. If one egg doesn't hatch or the first bird to hatch dies, the second offers another chance for reproductive success.

Although they resemble terns, tropicbirds are more closely related to pelicans and gannets. The **Red-billed Tropicbird** has one of the longest tails in the bird world, which it uses in aerial courtship and pair-formation displays, here near a nest site on the Galapagos. As it flies above the nest area, the bird gyrates and vocalizes. Tropicbirds are extremely agile and powerful fliers, able to forage more than fifty miles out to sea. Graceful as they may be while in the air, their landings are terribly awkward.

The distinct plumage of immature **Black-legged Kittiwakes** *(above)* sets them apart from all other species that nest near their colony, as does their distinctive, buoyant flight. The bird's light weight allows it to swoop around a cliff face with an agility gulls don't possess. Unlike many cliff-nesting birds, kittiwakes construct a deep, bowl-shaped nest anchored to a cliff. The nest is lined with grasses and seaweed. Kittiwake colonies can be enormous: one at Cape Saint Mary's contains more than a thousand nesting pairs, along with gannets, murres, razorbills, and other colonial nesters.

The gray, misting ocean and huge, crashing waves of St. Paul Island off Alaska create a scenic backdrop for seabird colonies. Despite this beauty, the cliffside colonies of the **Red-faced Cormorant** *(left)* are filthy places. Because there is much more vertical space than horizontal space, feces, the remains of partially eaten fish and crabs, even dead chicks, quickly blanket the ledges. Birds roosting below the others are often hit with whatever falls from above.

Seashore

WHEN WE THINK OF THE SEASHORE WE ENVISION TERNS DIVING FOR FISH, EGRETS WADING SHALLOW back bays, gulls resting on the waves, sandpipers scurrying across mudflats, waterfowl groping the shallows for snails and other morsels. The concept that certain birds can be found at the seashore goes beyond the world of science; the term "seashore" is not found in most ecology texts. To most of us, however, the meaning of the word is obvious.

Most birders know which birds they will find at the seashore, when those birds will be there, and what they will be doing. The seashore attracts different birds throughout the year. In summer, tidal marshes are loaded with nesting gulls, terns, rails, salt sparrows, and others. In late summer and autumn, the nesting species are joined by shorebirds and waterfowl, sometimes in numbers so vast they cannot be counted. In winter, many of the summer birds migrate south, leaving the hardier species: waterfowl and some raptors and songbirds. Finally, the spring brings a procession of north-bound migrants along with seashore nesters.

The edge of the ocean and sea provides a narrow but rich strip of habitats: shallow nearshore waters, bays, sounds, barrier islands, beaches, sand dunes, tidal wetlands, mangrove swamps, and intertidal zones. The food sources available can be extremely rich. The marsh grasses and marine plants of the back bays support the food chain, attracting fish and supporting enormous shellfish populations. Consequently, these habitats support an interesting assemblage of birds that make their living in very different ways. Birds that eat fish, birds that seek crabs along sodbanks in the marsh, birds that probe the mud for saltwater worms, and birds that eat other birds or mammals are attracted to the seashore's abundance of food. Each species has a unique set of adaptations that helps it harvest the bounty of its home.

Seashore habitats are frequently used by humans as vacation sites and so have come under enormous pressure in recent years. Beach-nesting birds like skimmers and terns now find few places where humans do not intrude, or where cats, foxes, crows, and gulls do not rob nests and eat young. Migrant shorebirds are constantly driven from their peaceful resting or foraging places. Terns and other fish-eaters are sometimes deprived of food because of overharvesting or pollution. For many species, life along the seashore is not as easy as it once was.

As well, a new threat to seashore birds is emerging: rising sea levels due to global warming. As the world's oceans rise at a historically unprecedented rate, the demise of beaches, sandspits, and salt marshes is imminent. Homes, roads, and other development close to the tide line exacerbate the problem, preventing beaches and marshes from migrating inland, as they've done for millennia. Bird habitat caught between rising oceans and man-made structures will be squeezed out, and birds that depend on seashore habitats will surely be affected. Whether these birds can adapt to the changes remains to be seen.

It is rare to see a shorebird like a **Lesser Yellowlegs** eating fish; they usually feed on small invertebrates: sand fleas, larval crabs, insect larvae, and the like. Shorebirds are very opportunistic during migration, however, taking whatever food they can. With the changing tides come varying feeding opportunities for shorebirds. Here, on the shallow intertidal flats of Long Island, a tidal pool with only a few inches of water trapped hundreds of small minnows. A variety of shorebirds quickly congregated to take advantage of the unexpected smorgasbord. By eating only a few fish, the Lesser Yellowlegs can fill its stomach with much less effort than when it feeds on a meal of invertebrates.

The diversity of the size and shape of shorebird bills is staggering and seems to be an adaptation for feeding in different ways and places and on different prey items. The aptly named **Long-billed Curlew** has one of the most distinctive and longest of shorebird bills. Long, curved bills can probe into crevices in mudflats and marshes where fiddler crabs hide. They also can probe deep into soft mud to extract worms and other creatures that are seeking refuge there.

Patience rewards a **Black-bellied Plover** foraging on an intertidal flat on Long Island. After grabbing a small part of a sand worm, the plover tugs gently to extract the meal from its burrow. Pulling too hard will break the worm, but a constant, even pressure tires the prey until the plover can ease it from the sand. Unlike most shorebirds, Black-bellied Plovers are hardy enough to overwinter as far north as coastal British Columbia on the Pacific coast and Long Island on the Atlantic. While some plovers migrate to the tropics, the species lives along thousands of miles of coastline, wherever invertebrates that live in the intertidal zone are present year-round. A tuft of dune grass serves as a windbreak during a cold winter's day.

The rich golden and rusty brown upperparts of a **Sanderling** in breeding plumage make it one of the most attractive of "peeps." These quick-moving wave dodgers forage in about an inch of water along sandy beaches during their south- and northbound migrations. They scurry between the waves, furiously probing for invertebrates like tiny mull crabs and sand fleas that live only a few millimeters beneath the beach surface. Although they seem common, Sanderlings have experienced a greater than fifty percent population decline in the past twenty-five years. The reason for this dramatic and disturbing decline is not known.

Like terns and skimmers, **Piping Plovers** nest on open beaches. Unlike the others, they do not nest in colonies. Instead, their nests are somewhat isolated, usually situated where there is little disturbance. The nest is often nothing more than a depression in the sand or gravel on the beach or behind the dunes. Plover eggs are cryptically colored and blend with the substrate, so they are not obvious to predators when the parents are off the nest. Piping Plovers are the earliest of the beach nesters, coming back to the northeastern coast before winter ends. Early nesting allows them to lay a second clutch if the first is wiped out by a nor'easter or eaten by predators. Piping Plovers are one of the most critically endangered species in North America and have been wiped out from much of their range by man-made disturbances to their habitats. In the Midwest, for example, the channelization of the Missouri River has eliminated plover nesting islands, and the species has all but disappeared.

There is always action at a **Black Skimmer** colony, including numerous aerial displays of aggressive behavior. When one bird comes too close to the nest of another, it is quickly and loudly warned away. Such agonistic behavior is typical among colonial nesters; the territories within a colony are actually quite tiny, sometimes only a few square feet. There isn't much room available on a sandbar that's only a couple inches above the high-tide mark. Packing nests tightly serves a purpose, however. It helps the colony detect predators more easily.

The long legs and bill of the **Black-necked Stilt** are important adaptations for feeding. Because they can stand in relatively deep water, stilts are able to feed in places most other shorebirds can't. Here, a Black-necked Stilt feeds in the Salton Sea National Wildlife Refuge in southern California. Although the water is only a couple inches deep, it's deeper than most small sandpipers can handle. In the salty ponds and lakes of the West, tiny brine flies and brine shrimp make up a majority of the stilt's diet, but it is adept at taking a variety of food items.

The **Heermann's Gull** is lighter on the wing than many other gulls, enabling it to make tight radius turns, climb rapidly, and chase other birds with ease. Most importantly, these aerial abilities permit this bird to be piratic: its agility allows it to harass other species that have food until they drop their meal. On California beaches where Heermann's Gulls are found, other species must eat what they find quickly or face merciless harassment. Piratic behavior is found most often in wide-open habitats: over beaches, marshes, and the waters of the ocean.

Willets *(above)* are rather dull-looking birds, uniform in color, all drab shades of gray and brown. That is until they open their wings and flash their distinctive black-and-white markings. On the open salt marshes, beaches, and wet meadows where Willets nest, their wing markings can be seen at great distances. For a birder, these markings allow for quick identification. To other Willets, they are meaningful courtship or aggressive displays.

It is not immediately apparent why the bill of the **American Avocet** *(left)* is so long and upturned, until you see the bird feeding. Its bill shape and size are adaptations for a peculiar foraging behavior in fresh, brackish, and salt water. To catch crustaceans, aquatic insects, and vegetable material, the avocet sweeps its bill quickly from side to side, churning up the bottom and exposing tiny edibles, which the bird feels with its sensitive bill and quickly gobbles. This behavior is used whether the bird is feeding in the brackish water of a back bay on the Texas Gulf coast or on its freshwater nesting ponds in the Great Plains. Large expanses of open, shallow water are preferred.

The rocky beaches and jetties of the northeastern coast of North America are the winter homes of **Purple Sandpipers.** While most sandpipers find food on sand, mud, or grass, Purple Sandpipers prefer to feed near the rough waters of rocky shorelines. They work the water's edge, often only a few feet from crashing waves, picking arthropods and mollusks, moving from rock to rock. In the winter, the birds deftly scramble over surfaces coated with slick ice. Contrary to its name, the Purple Sandpiper is not really purple, and it rarely sets foot on the sand.

Long-billed Dowitchers love to forage on mudflats and in shallow pools and wet meadows. Their long, soft bills allow them to probe deeply for crustaceans, mollusks, and worms that dwell beneath the surface. At times while feeding, dowitchers will venture into breast-deep water and dunk their heads completely under to probe the mud. Rapid, repetitious, "sewing-machine" bobbing is characteristic of this species. The rust-colored breeding plumage of the Long-billed Dowitcher lasts only from early spring through mid-summer. Birders in the temperate zone do not see this plumage for long; spring migrants pass through more quickly than they do in the fall. In late summer, when dowitchers and most other shorebirds move south from their arctic nesting grounds, their beautiful breeding plumage has faded to drabber browns and grays.

Almost from the time they hatch, **Mew Gull** chicks can walk. This precocial nature is common among ground-nesting birds like gulls and shorebirds that breed in exposed habitats. The ability to leave the nest, walk, and swim almost immediately after hatching reduces the chances of predation by mammals and other birds. Mew Gulls that nest on gravel and sandbars of rivers and the edges of lakes and ponds are actually semiprecocial, quickly taking to the water at the approach of coyotes and other enemies. Unlike truly precocial birds, they remain near the nest and are not able to feed themselves for several weeks. Young gulls scream for food, their primary activity when they are just a few days old.

Unlike precocial or semiprecocial beach nesters, newly hatched **Least Tern** chicks are completely helpless. After hatching, adults stay with the chicks most of the time to protect them from predators and shade them from the sun and rain. Both eggs and chicks are camouflaged and not easily seen against the sand and gravel of a beach. After the eggs have hatched, adult terns don't necessarily use the same scrape in the sand as their nest. If threatened by high tides or predators, they will move their chicks to a new scrape. The young remain in the nest for about three weeks; even after they venture out, their parents continue to feed them. Vulnerable is the only way to describe Least Terns' nesting habitat. This is, in part, why the bird is endangered over much of its range. On the coasts of the United States, terns nest on beaches along the ocean or bays and sounds. In the interior, the nests are often situated on sandbars along rivers or lakes. The nests—little more than a slight depression in the ground—are extremely vulnerable to flooding, which can wipe out an entire tern colony. Beach development has resulted in increased disturbance by humans and predation by cats and dogs. Fortunately, the species seems to fare well when colonies are fenced off to keep beach walkers away.

A head-up display reveals the marvelous color pattern of the **Brown Pelican's** gular pouch, which serves many important functions. This bird is in peak breeding plumage, and the red coloration of the gular area is undoubtedly a signal associated with pair formation and bonding. It may even be a signal that triggers copulation. The pelican's pouch also serves as a means of capturing and holding fish and as a way to keep cool: fluttering the pouch causes air to pass over the moist interior, speeding evaporation and dissipating body heat.

After decades of DDT and other pesticide poisoning, the **Osprey** nearly disappeared from the United States and southern Canada. Now Ospreys are once again becoming familiar nesters in salt marshes and along seashores. With a wingspan of just under six feet, the bird is hard to miss. Their nests are also conspicuous: large and bulky, often six feet in diameter, two feet tall, and weighing more than a hundred pounds. Traditional nesting sites are used by several generations of Ospreys. Hundreds of man-made nesting platforms have helped increase the population of this troubled species.

For **Common Terns,** eating requires an almost constant tour of vast expanses of ocean and back bays in search of a school of silversides or bay anchovies. When a school is found, the terns hover above it, looking down, waiting for the prey to get close to the water's surface. Frequently, predatory fish will drive the smaller baitfish to the surface by the thousands, offering terns a welcome opportunity for an easy meal. To feed, terns dive headfirst, often crashing into the water from heights of twenty feet or more. They try to grab the prey with their bills and quickly take flight. Not every attempt is successful; young terns must sometimes dive for hours before they capture their quarry.

Laughing Gulls (*above*) usually swallow their prey whole. If they don't, another gull will probably try to steal it. This Gulf Butterfish, however, was a bit too big. It had to be pecked to pieces before it could be eaten. Laughing Gulls can eat an enormous variety of foods. They flock to schools of fish and other seafood in marshes and coastal waters. They dive and swoop through swarms of insects, sometimes gorging for hours. They raid garbage cans, follow farmers plowing fields, even steal burgers off the grill. On the beaches of the Delaware Bay, thousands of Laughing Gulls gather in May to feed on horseshoe-crab eggs, sometimes pushing aside the migrating shorebirds that depend on this rich resource.

Except for the nesting season, **Short-billed Dowitchers** (*left*), like most shorebirds, live with others of their species or mix with other species of shorebirds. Hundreds of dowitchers and other shorebirds converging as an orchestrated unit on food-rich tidal mudflats or shallow freshwater pools are a common sight. The flocks are largest at migration stopovers during autumn. Although being part of a flock results in competition for food, there are several advantages for members of a flock. Most importantly, a flock has more eyes, which are better for detecting predators—a nearby Merlin or Peregrine Falcon, for example. Individuals in a flock can spend less time looking for predators and more time looking for food.

The salt marshes that host **Saltmarsh Sharp-tailed Sparrows** and other salt sparrows are not graced with many places to perch. For a sparrow to get a good view of its surroundings or a place to utter its buzzy song, it must be part gymnast, making do with marsh grasses and a few woody plants. Sharp-tails are adept at using cordgrass and spikerush as perching places—at least for brief periods of time. To stay exposed for too long might attract the attention of a harrier or other predator or advertise the presence of a nest.

This **Ruddy Turnstone** is probably disappointed that there is no food in this horseshoe-crab carapace. Although turnstones normally eat tiny invertebrates, during May along the Delaware Bay, when horseshoe crabs emerge from the water to lay their eggs in the sand, tens of thousands of turnstones join in a hyperphagic binge that involves nearly a million birds. Among Red Knots, Sanderlings, and Semipalmated Sandpipers feasting on the bounty, Ruddy Turnstones are the real excavators, often digging an inch or more in the sand to uncover globs of eggs. The annual egg-eating extravaganza is vitally important to these shorebirds, allowing them to fatten up in preparation for the final leg of their migration back to the tundra. A feeding Ruddy Turnstone resembles a pig. With a bill proportionately shorter than most sandpipers' and sometimes turning upward, the turnstone roots through debris and stones looking for food. It is one of the few shorebirds that turns objects—seaweed and shells, as well as stones—to reveal invertebrate goodies underneath.

Species List

Arctic Tundra

Page 2: Arctic Tern (*Sterna paradisea*), Nome, AK

Page 3: Pacific Golden-Plover (*Pluvialis fulva*), Nome, AK

Page 4: Pacific Loon (*Gavia pacifica*), Churchill, Manitoba

Page 5: Peregrine Falcon (*Falco Peregrinus*), Long Island, NY

Page 6: American Golden-Plover (*Pluvialis dominica*), Churchill, Manitoba

Page 7: Snowy Owl (*Nyctea scandiaca*), Long Island, NY

Page 8: Red-necked Phalarope (*Phalaropus lobatus*), Churchill, Manitoba; Nome, AK

Page 9: Yellow Wagtail (*Motacilla flava*), Nome, AK

Page 10: Red-throated Loon (*Gavia stellata*), Nome, AK

Page 11: Arctic Warbler (*Phylloscopus borealis*), Nome, AK

Page 12: Bonaparte's Gull (*Larus philadelphia*), Churchill, Manitoba

Page 13: Bluethroat, (*Luscinia svecica*), Nome, AK

Page 14: Smith's Longspur (*Calcarius pictus*), Churchill, Manitoba

Page 15: Northern Shrike (*Lanius excubitor*), Nome, AK

Page 15: Gyrfalcon (*Falco rusticolus*), Nome, AK

Page 16: Ruddy Turnstone (*Arenaria interpres*), Nome, AK

Page 16: Western Sandpiper (*Calidris mauri*), Nome, AK

Page 17: Willow Ptarmigan (*Lagopus lagopus*), Churchill, Manitoba

Page 18: Willow and Rock ptarmigan (*Lagopus lagopus* and *Lagopus mutus*), Churchill, Manitoba

Page 19: Winter Wren (*Troglodytes troglodytes*), St. Paul Island, Pribilofs, AK

Page 19: Savannah Sparrow (*Passerculus sandwichensis*), Nome, AK

Page 20: Long-tailed Jaeger (*Stercorarius longicaudus*), Nome, AK

Page 20: Parasitic Jaeger (*Stercorarius parasiticus*), Churchill, Manitoba

Page 21: Ross's Gull (*Rhodostethia rosea*), Churchill, Manitoba

Page 22: Dunlin (*Calidris alpina*), Churchill, Manitoba

Page 23: Stilt Sandpiper (*Calidris himantopus*), Churchill, Manitoba

Page 23: Short-billed Dowitcher (*Limnodromus griseus*), Churchill, Manitoba

Page 24: Rock Sandpiper (*Calidris ptilocnemis*), Nome, AK

Page 25: Lapland Longspur (*Calcarius lapponicus*), Nome, AK

Page 26: Hudsonian Godwit (*Limosa haemastica*), Churchill, Manitoba

Page 27: Snow Bunting (*Plectrophenax nivalis*), St. Paul Island, Pribilofs, AK

Page 28: Canada Goose (*Branta canadensis*), Churchill, Manitoba

Page 28: Northern Wheatear (*Oenanthe oenanthe*), Nome, AK

Forest and Field

Page 30: Barn Owl (*Tyto alba*), rehab center

Page 31: Northern Goshawk (*Accipiter gentilis*), VT

Page 31: Painted Bunting (*Passerina ciris*), southern TX

Page 32: Mountain Bluebird (*Sialia currucoides*), MT

Page 32: Golden-crowned Kinglet (*Regulus satrapa*), Long Island, NY

Page 33: Anna's Hummingbird (*Calypte anna*), CA

Page 34: Eastern Bluebird (*Sialia sialis*), Jessup, PA

Page 35: Sharp-shinned Hawk (*Accipiter striatus*), Cape May, NJ

Page 35: Cooper's Hawk (*Accipiter cooperii*), Cape May, NJ

Page 36: Northern Saw-whet Owl (*Aegolius acadicus*), Long Island, NY

Page 37: Hermit Thrush (*Catharus guttatus*), Long Island, NY

Page 37: White-throated Sparrow (*Zonotrichia albicollis*), Long Island, NY

Page 38: Baltimore Oriole (*Icterus galbula*), Long Island, NY

Page 39: Northern Cardinal (*Cardinalis cardinalis*), Long Island, NY

Page 39: Scarlet Tanager (*Piranga olivacea*), Long Island, NY

Page 40: Yellow Warbler (*Dendroica petechia*), Point Pelee, Ontario

Page 40: Common Yellowthroat (*Geothlypis trichas*), Long Island, NY

Page 41: Northern Parula (*Parula americana*), Long Island, NY

Page 42: Tree Swallow (*Tachycineta bicolor*), Long Island, NY

Page 43: Purple Martin (*Progne subis*), Crane Creek, OH

Page 44: Florida Scrub-Jay (*Aphelocoma coerulescens*), central FL

Page 45: Red-bellied Woodpecker (*Melanerpes carolinus*), Long Island, NY

Page 45: Northern Flicker (*Colaptes auratus*), Long Island, NY

Photographer's Note

THE SIGHT OF A FALCON HUNTING ITS PREY, THE GRACEFUL FLIGHT OF AN EGRET, OR THOUSANDS OF snow geese taking off at sunrise is just part of what motivates me to photograph birds. Their exquisite colors, shapes, and textures capture my eye, and their actions, habits, and habitats interest me as well. The avian world fascinates me, and I love to document it on film.

What's amazing about bird photography is that I can photograph the same species of bird a thousand times and never expose the same image. There are many variables that make an image different, and every time I'm out shooting the situation is unique. The birds may be in different plumage, the backgrounds and habitat always vary. Changes in lighting and weather conditions can alter the whole feeling of a photo as well. I'm constantly hunting and creating circumstances for an image that is new and different. Contending with all these variables is what makes my job so fascinating.

In the fourteen years I've spent birding and photographing I was always curious about the birds' behavior and wanted to learn more about how these beautiful animals live. This is what prompted the idea for this book. Many times while I'm taking pictures of a bird, I wonder why it's acting in a certain way, or what it eats, or where it migrates. Many questions that I have still remain unanswered. This mystery intrigues me. So I thought a book that featured information about the behavior of the birds I have photographed through the years would make a worthwhile project.

To create my bird photography, I've traveled many miles to the most wondrous places. I consider myself very lucky to have the opportunity to commune with nature as I do. It's not only the birds that I treasure, it's also being out there enjoying all of what nature has to offer.

The photos in this book were taken with various Nikon equipment, including Nikon F4 and F5 camera bodies and the 600mm f4D ED-IF AF-S Nikkor lens, with and without the TC-14E 1.4X teleconverter. Other lenses used were the Nikkor 500mm f4D AF-I, the 300mm f2.8 AF-I, the 200mm f4D AF micro, the 80–200mm f2.8D IF-ED AF-S Zoom, and the 24–120 f3.5–5.6D AF Zoom. Some of the flight shots were taken with a Canon A2 camera body and the Canon 400mm 5.6 autofocus lens. I used a Gitzo 1549 carbon-fiber tripod with a Foba Superball tripod head. My choice of film was Fujichrome Velvia for most of the portraits. I also used Provia F 100 pushed to 200 for many of the action shots, especially the flight photos. All of my film was processed at Chelsea Professional Services in New York.

Some of my favorite photo techniques include using blinds with feeding set-ups, or just blinds out in the wild; shooting from a vehicle, using a beanbag or window mount to keep the camera steady; and sitting in a kayak with a tripod mounted in front of me. I also enjoy hiking and scanning the landscape for great photo opportunities.

None of the photos in this book were computer enhanced or manipulated in any way. The Barn Owl on page 30 and Northern Goshawk on page 31 were taken at raptor rehabilitation centers. All of us involved with this project decided to include these images to illustrate interesting facts.